My husband,

Next Door

By

T. Marie

Text copyright © 2016 by T. Marie

All Rights Reserved

This book and the effort involved
is dedicated to
God for my strength
and to my children for their continued
laughter, love and support.

Table of Contents

Chapter 1
Chapter 2
Chapter 3
Chapter 4
Chapter 5
Chapter 6
Chapter 7
Chapter 8
Chapter 9
Chapter 10
Chapter 11
Chapter 12
Chapter 13
Chapter 14
Chapter 15
Chapter 16
Chapter 17
Chapter 18
Chapter 19
Chapter 20
Chapter 21
Chapter 22
Chapter 23
Chapter 24
Chapter 25
Chapter 26
Chapter 27
Chapter 28
Chapter 29
Chapter 30
Epilogue

Chapter 1

Five minutes seems like forever when taking a pregnancy test, thought Cassidy. She was planning on letting Jamie know but didn't want him to stress her out even more than she already was during the waiting process of five whole minutes. He definitely could be impatient. He seemed distracted lately but she figured it was probably due to his work and the pressures of his most recent promotion. Often his distraction could be so extreme Cassidy would pretend she was married to someone else. Maybe someone she dated in college, a cute co-worker, anyone really. Just so long as they talked to her at the dinner table, shared the events of their day, asked how her day was, maybe surprise her with flowers or even an impromptu kiss every so often. Was that too much to ask? Had it always been this way with Jamie?

Cassidy thought back to a time when he was attentive and loving and even funny. Although she can't recall the last time they laughed together. They did watch old sitcoms together and she remembered watching Cheers about a month ago and both were laughing pretty good at Norm and Cliff and some of the things they said. That was a good night. They had delicious take-out from their favorite Chinese restaurant, Mr. Lee's, and shared a bottle of wine. Maybe two. She couldn't recall if they were celebrating something or that somehow they just ended up having a good night together. But they did. Actually, she realized, that evening was the night in question and the reason she was taking a pregnancy test. Cassidy sighed and snapped back to the present, her test ready to read.

Cassidy picked up the box to be sure to know what the signs meant even though it was probably an obvious sign. Sure enough, a pink plus sign meant pregnant and a pink negative sign meant not pregnant. Easy enough but she was nervous. Her hand was shaking as she brought the test closer to her face to read the sign. She held her breath and suddenly held the test strip to the side to not look directly at it and *slowly* moved it in front of her face to see. What she saw was a plus sign. She exhaled. She didn't move. She stared at the plus sign. The positive sign. Whoa.

The silence in the bathroom was deafening. Cassidy wondered if she was happy or indifferent and the hesitation concerned her. Her first thought was of Jamie and how he can either make this the happiest moment in her life or not. Her second thought was that, yes, no matter what, *she* really was happy. And she would not let him take that away from her regardless of how he reacted.

Cassidy suddenly heard the front door open and muffled voices downstairs. She quickly, and for no reason really, hid the pregnancy test evidence and went downstairs to find her best friend, and neighbor, Cindy, talking with Jamie in the living room. She looked like she had been crying.

"Cin, what's wrong?" Cassie went over to Cindy and hugged her. When she pulled back she saw Jamie off to the side but ignored him.

"Well," she sniffed, "Bob and I are over," Cindy said sadly. Cassidy knew Cindy wasn't completely happy lately and blamed it on Bob's extensive work travels for his job as a Director of Sales for a large pharmaceutical company. Although when he was home he was very loving and affectionate towards Cindy. Sometimes Cass wished Jamie were more like Bob in that respect. Cassidy asked Cindy many times throughout the past few months how things were and shared her concerns that it seemed like something was wrong but Cindy always said things were fine and that she was just tired. Cindy could definitely be dramatic and even high maintenance at times so Cass never pushed it and let it go, but here she was saying it was over with the two of them.

"When did this happen? How? Why?" asked Cassidy. Jamie was silent and looked uncomfortable as many men stuck in the same room as a crying woman can be. But Cass still didn't want to think about him right now especially with her best friend falling apart in front of her.

Cindy sniffled again and wiped her nose. Even with a red nose and red eyes Cindy was a knockout. One of those naturally pretty people with the thick wavy hair that air dried perfectly, olive skin and a gorgeous smile. *She won't be on the market long*, thought Cassidy. It would be weird to someday have a new man in their neighborly group living next door.

"It just happened. It's been a long time coming. I told Bob it was over. We talked for a long time but my mind's made up. He took some things and went to a hotel. He just came back from a conference so he still had a packed suitcase. I guess my timing was good so he was able to leave right away," said Cindy. She started to shake her head a little and stood up straighter.

Cassie thought she heard anger creep into Cindy's voice as she described how Bob left so soon. She suddenly didn't seem as sad anymore. Cassie thought that was kind of strange but figured Cindy was mad at Bob. She wasn't sure why they were breaking up so maybe Bob cheated on Cindy or something. She doubted that. Bob didn't seem the type but you never knew for sure. Cassie had definitely heard enough stories of infidelity to know that things happen.

"But what actually happened to lead to this?" Cassie asked. "I knew things were a little off with you two but not that off. I'm sorry to be so nosey but none of this makes any sense," Cassidy said with disbelief and curiosity.

Jamie was still in the room looking uncomfortable and Cassidy noticed Cindy and he were sharing quick glances. Cassidy realized Cindy probably didn't want to talk about the details with Jamie around nor did Jamie want to be in this situation. Jamie, being a guy after all, didn't like topics unless they included sports or in Jamie's case, trees. Jamie loved trees. He enjoyed going on long drives in the country to see different ones and had a few coffee table books about his favorite types of trees. Cassie always wondered why but they never talked about his tree obsession. When they first bought their house he planted a Malus Hybrid tree in the front yard. That's what he called it to anyone who admired its fuchsia colored leaves. They always had him repeat the name. To the average person, it was a crabapple tree. He also planted a Quercus towards the side of the house. An oak tree.

"Jamie, why don't you go on upstairs and let me talk to Cindy in private," said Cassidy.

"Oh, umm, no, umm, I want to stay," Jamie stammered. He looked over at Cindy and she nodded. What the- ?

"Cassidy," said Cindy firmly with a sudden lack of sniffling or sadness. "We have to tell you something."

"Umm, okay…" Cassidy said with a Jamie-like stammer. "What's going on?" During their talk they had migrated into the kitchen. Cassie had been about to make some tea for them but stopped and leaned back against the kitchen counter.

"The reason things are over with Bob and I is because Jamie and I are in love," said Cindy ever so confident and bitch-like. The room suddenly seemed to be sucked of all the air. Cassidy felt like she was hit by a mac truck, in slow motion. She couldn't move, she literally could not react. She was unable to blink, swallow, step to the right to slap Jamie or step to the left to haul ass on Cindy.

After a few moments of staring at the two of them, Cassie asked, "What are you talking about? Is this a joke?"

Cindy and Jamie looked at each other again and then Jamie looked down at the ground while Cindy kept pushing the knife in Cassie's back.

"This is not a joke," Cindy proclaimed as if spreading the Good Word. "Jamie and I have had feelings for each other for about a year now and we didn't want to act on them because of you and Bob. But," she looked over at Jamie and held his eyes before continuing, "…our love for each other is so strong that we couldn't take it anymore so we finally gave in and here we are."

Cindy turned back to look at Cassidy but not before giving Jamie a cheesy smile that make Cassie want to throw up. "We hope you understand and that we can –."

But Cindy couldn't finish her sentence because of her stunned reaction to being slapped by Cassidy. "You bitch," said Cassie with perfect articulation. "How dare you come into my home and even THINK my husband is anything more than MY HUSBAND! He is a married, off the market man!" Even as Cassie was going off on Cindy, she knew that many married men were still ON the market. She knew her words were empty attempts of trying to stand up for what she felt was right and for her marriage. And to surprisingly defend Jamie's infidelity.

Cindy stood there holding her hand on her face. She was speechless.

"Um, Cass, it was, uh, mutual so not all her fault," said stupid Jamie. He started to step towards Cindy but stopped in his tracks when he saw the look on Cassie's face.

"Shut. Up. Ass. Hole," Cassidy said in a voice she didn't recognize as her own. She stepped toward him and he took a step back. A quick one. Coward. "How dare you do this to me, to our marriage, our life?!"

"Oh, Cass," said Cindy, over her shock of being appropriately bitch slapped. "You two fight all the time so why are you so surprised?" Cindy waved her hand as if casting Cassie's feelings to the side. Cassie just couldn't believe how bold and rude Cindy was being. She couldn't believe anything she was seeing or hearing.

"Oh, I don't know, Cindy, because all couples fight and because I thought Jamie and I would get back to a good place. I didn't realize he had already *checked out* with my best friend that I confided in! How convenient for you to know our issues! No wonder you never gave *any* advice and just listened to me. You were probably so giddy inside while I was pouring my heart out to you! How can you even look at yourself in the mirror?"

Cassidy started to shake a little and was suddenly exhausted. She didn't know what else to say or do. The bottom line was that her husband cheated on her with her best friend and neighbor. He admitted it. It was over. Her marriage was over. What do they do now? She had planned on making chicken for dinner. Does he go over to Cindy's house tonight and sleep in her bed? Does she still make the chicken? Cassie was simply unable to form a sensible thought.

"Well, you seem too worked up to talk to now, Cass, and there really isn't anything left to say. So Jamie and I are going to get out of here," said Cindy with a flare of drama. "Let's go Jamie."

Jamie stood still for a few moments while Cassidy and Cindy watched him. Cindy looked at him impatiently and Cassidy looked at him with a great deal of confusion and sadness.

Jamie looked at both of them briefly and finally started to walk towards the front door, grabbing his overnight bag strategically placed in the foyer and briefcase next to it on his way out. He paused with his back to the women. Cassie could tell he didn't want to look back at her. That he did feel bad that he hurt her. But obviously he didn't feel bad enough to ask forgiveness and stay with her. To maybe try to make things right.

"Oh, one more thing…Jamie and I are pregnant," said Cindy. And with that she and Jamie left and an extremely shocked Cassidy stood in the silence of her living room, her mouth hanging open, wonder what the f- just happened.

Chapter 2

The next morning Cassidy woke up with a horrible headache. She barely slept and hadn't eaten anything since lunch the day before and wasn't even hungry. She had to get to work for a 9 am meeting that she was heading up and still needed to make copies of various items to pass around.

As she lay there thinking of all she needed to do it suddenly hit her, again, that her marriage was over. And then another thought hit her like a smack in the head, she was pregnant! *What kind of mother am I going to be if I've already forgotten I'm pregnant*, she thought?

Cassie slowly got out of bed, used the bathroom, took some headache medicine, and went downstairs to find something to eat. Wait, is she able to take medicine for a headache? There were so many things on her mind so she grabbed a pad of paper and started to write down a list of things to do while she stood at the kitchen counter. Make appointment with OBGYN. Make appointment with divorce lawyer. Go to the bank and move money around. How sad. She never could have imagined writing a list like this.

She was starting to get mad and her anger was taking over the hazy confusion that has been her mental state for the past 12 hours or so. And her appetite started to come back. Cassidy made some toast and drank a glass of orange juice, figuring it would be good for the baby. The baby. And Jamie didn't even know. *One more thing to add to the list*, she thought.

Cassidy got to work around 8 am and started making copies for the meeting. She felt better and headache free. She enjoyed being at the office. It was a place where she felt in control. She was a Project Manager so that added to her feeling good but she also felt like someone who was able to take care of herself. Throughout the years she grew to feel strong inside and had put a large focus on her career. Maybe if she hadn't been so focused on her career she would have noticed what was going on with Jamie. But, at the same time, she didn't want to take any blame for his cheating on her. Yet, she was smart enough to know that there are two sides to every story. Maybe she ignored him when she had big projects to work on. Or maybe she turned him down too many times when he wanted to be intimate. She didn't know. Maybe she would never know.

But, regardless, she was thankful she had a good job in a nice office with a solid and growing company. Given the change of events that were about to happen to her in this sudden new life, she felt confident that she would be able to provide for herself and her baby. There were a lot of things to still work out and she was definitely heartbroken, but this moment of peace was welcoming. As she waited for copies to finish her co-worker, Joe, came in with a grin on his face.

"Hey, pretty lady, getting ready for the big meeting?" Even though Joe was asking about Cassidy he seemed to not really care how she was and looked like he was dying to tell her something.

"Yeah, yes, almost there," she turned to check on the copies to make sure they weren't falling all over the floor as they often did. "So what's up with you?"

"Well... I'm in love!!!!!!" Joe cried loudly and twirled around the copy room. Yes, Joe was a twirler.

"With....?" Cass asked slowly.

Joe gave Cassie an annoyed look. "Jack! Duh. Remember, I had my date with him last night? We finally decided to meet each other? The one I've been talking to for weeks on one of my dating sites?" He was eager for her to remember and thankfully she did.

"Oh, right! Sorry, I had a rough night. I'm glad you two finally got together! So, you love him, huh? What is he like? How did the date go?" Cassie's copies were done and she needed to sort them but didn't want to be rude. She turned her full attention to Joe as he started to tell her about his night with Jack.

"He is sooo dreamy. As you know," he clapped his hands together, "he's a lawyer with a very good career. We had such an easy conversation during dinner and then went for ice cream afterwards. We both love ice cream!" He said this as if they were the only two people in the world who liked ice cream and had finally found each other.

"We had parked in the SAME parking lot without knowing it so we were able to walk back to our cars together! He kissed me good night and said he wanted to see me again! Yay!!!!" Joe was so excited he started to jump up and down while clapping his hands fast and close together. Cassidy was really happy for him. His past few relationships were with real losers and each one ended badly so it was good to see him act this way.

"That's great! I'm so happy for you!" She hugged him tight. "Listen, I don't mean to cut you off but my copies are finished and I have to get things in order for the meeting. Maybe we can go to lunch today? My treat. I want to hear more about Jack and I have some news of my own."

"Okay, sounds good. I have a client coming in soon and need to get ready, too. Good luck at your meeting!"

They quickly hugged again and Cassie hurried to her office to check emails and voice mails. Her cell phone pinged and she saw it was a message from Jamie. Ugh. What the hell does he want? His stupid text read that he needed to stop by and grab some more things so planned to do that while she was at work today. What a thoughtful idiot. She replied for him to be out of there before she got home and then added another quick text saying she needed to talk to him, alone, to go over a few things. Faster than the speed of light he responded with an "Okay." Whatever, asshole.

The meeting went off well. Cassidy's boss, Stuart Sandor, seemed happy with her presentation and the rest of her team gave some good input, too. She delegated some of the things that needed to be done and left a good portion to herself as this project was her baby. Well, her *other* baby, and she wanted to do a good job for the potential client as well for her job security now that she was soon to be a single parent. Cassidy went back to her office, sat at her desk and exhaled. The meeting had been on her mind more than she realized. She was glad it was over. While she loved her job it definitely came with a good amount of pressure.

When she first interviewed at the company she was fresh out of college and oblivious to life. But she had a Marketing Degree and interviewed well and eventually received her first real job offer. Her starting salary was a lot more than a college student was used to but not as much as she'd hoped for when she dreamt about being in the work force. But her parents gave her the best advice she ever received. They told her she had to pay her dues. She had to start somewhere, put the time in, work hard and make a good impression. It was probably the best advice she ever received. Too many people she knew at that college graduate age felt entitled and didn't want to learn and put the time in with a lesser paying role. They wanted it all at that moment. Cassie was glad, even then, to not feel that way for long. She took the job and had to learn how to manage her money but eventually she got the hang of it and with hard work received a few promotions along the way which strengthened her career and position at the company. Overall she learned a lot about life that they hadn't taught in school.

Later that day, Joe and Cassidy met at a hip new café across the street from the office. It wasn't necessarily Cassie's preferred place to eat but it's location to their office made it an easy choice. The place had a high energy vibe with small tables, couches and a bar area and loud noises of dishes clanking around and alternative music. She would have been in serious pain if she still had that headache. Joe was a few minutes late but it gave Cassidy time to figure out how to tell him of her latest events. The waitress took their drink orders and they looked over the menu. Cassidy spotted a few people from the office and waved. The waitress was back and took their food orders and finally it was time.

"So, what is this big news you have to tell me?" asked Joe.

"Well, I actually have two big pieces of news… The first is… I'm pregnant." She realized she told him this without exclamation. Almost as if she was waiting for his approval. Joe didn't seem to notice and after pausing for a moment he jumped out of his seat to hug her. They laughed and she became teary eyed, Joe noticing when he sat back down.

"That is great, Cass. It really is. I know you and Jamie had talked about starting a family but it seemed so long ago that you were excited to actually start one. I don't mean to be rude, but, are you happy? You didn't really deliver the news with excitement…"

"I am happy. I really am," she said while looking down at her napkin, twisting it in her hands. "But, like I said, I have two pieces of news. The second is that," she looked Joe in the eye and continued, "… Jamie cheated on me and we're getting a divorce." There, it was out. It felt good to unload this on someone. Joe sat there speechless which was not a common occurrence for him.

"What? Why? What?" he stammered.

"I know. He's apparently been having an affair with Cindy."

"What? Why? When?" Joe wasn't an English major.

Tears started to come to Cassidy's eyes. She looked down again and Joe reached across the table for her hand. The waitress came with the food, they always timed things like that so well, and asked if they needed anything else. Joe replied they were all good and she left to check on her other tables.

"I am so sorry, Cass. How did you find out? When did you find out?"

Cassidy replayed the last night's events for Joe and he nodded and said "shit" and "no way" in all the right places. Once she was done they both picked at their food quietly. After a bit of time they both started to eat and small talked about things at the office. She liked how this was going. She got it off her chest, told one of her best friends, and they easily changed the subject so she could compose herself.

Once their meals were finished they went outside into the warm sunshine and walked to a nearby park bench away from the crowd. Co-workers were all around and she didn't really want to talk to anyone except Joe. She and Joe talked a bit longer and Cassidy let the tears come freely since no one was around and she had sunglasses on, too.

Joe knew better than to offer any advice but did say she needed to make one of her famous "to-do lists" and jot down things as they came to her mind. He knew her so well. She felt so much better after talking to him. They walked back to the office with her arm linked in his, ready to finish the work day and get home to unwind on a Friday night. Oh, and deal with the moron.

Chapter 3

Cassidy had driven home from work thousands of times but this was the first time she was nervous. She did not like the feeling. Her home was her home. Yes, she had made it with Jamie but for the past few months she was growing used to his travels and late nights at the office so their home seemed less theirs and more hers. But regardless, she knew he lived there and his stuff was all over. And the two big trees he loved were the first things she saw as she drove closer to the house. This time she started to tear up over the trees. She really needed to get a grip. Maybe she should consider selling and buying a smaller house. With no trees. Ugh. One thing at a time. She'd add it to her to-do list. Maybe.

No cars were in her driveway, or Cindy's. Good. Maybe the happy couple wasn't around, she hoped. Cassie just wanted to get in the garage and lock herself in the house. She came in through the garage door that led her to the main hallway of the downstairs. Her cat, a tabby named Sophie, ran up to her and purred at her feet. She bent down to pet her and rub behind her ears, Sophie's favorite spot.

"Hey, Soph, are you hungry?" Sophie let out a loud meow. "I'll take that as a 'hell yes!' Okay, let's get you fed."

Cassie stood back up, took her coat off and put her keys and briefcase on the table. She saw a pile of mail sitting there she had been ignoring so made a mental note to go through it to make sure no bills were hiding. Which they probably were.

She fed Sophie and checked the fridge to see what her choices were for dinner. She still had a package of chicken thawed out with the intent, from the night before, to make it for dinner for her and Jamie. Now, it was simply too much chicken for one person. This thought, sadly and oddly, brought tears to her eyes. Again. She numbly sat down on a kitchen chair, put her elbows on the table, held her head in her hands and cried.

About an hour later, after washing her face, cleaning up the house and getting laundry sorted, she prepared and put in the oven a healthy meal of baked chicken breast lightly seasoned, baked potatoes and green beans covered in foil. Cassidy sat back down at the kitchen table with a cup of decaf tea and her list of things to do. She made more food than she needed, not wanting to waste all the chicken, but figured she could have the extras for lunch the next day. Did they even sell chicken for one?

Sophie purred against her leg and jumped on the table then sat on Cassie's "to do" list. Cass petted her for a bit and then heard the front door being rattled, almost as if someone were trying to open it and come inside. If that was Jamie she was going to beat his ass. She darted for the front window and looked to the side. The porch light was out, neither she nor Jamie had replaced it yet, so it was hard to see who was there.

Sure enough a man was looking at the door as if it were an object that had suddenly stepped in his way. Sensing someone looking at him he turned and looked directly at Cassie, making her jump back. She heard her name being called and realized it was Brian, Jamie's brother. Crap. She had no choice but to let him in. She opened the door and was suddenly enveloped in one of Brian's drunken bear hugs.

"Cass-eh-dyyyy!! My fav'rit sister in law," Brian slightly slurred.

"Hey Brian, what's going on?" She helped him inside and shut the door before Sophie ran out. Brian started taking off his sports coat and looking around the foyer as if seeing it for the first time. Cassidy had seen Brian drunk in college on more than one occasion but not too many times after graduation. He went on to law school and she and Jamie didn't see him that much except for holidays and an occasional birthday party. Once he passed the bar, Brian received a job offer from a company he had done an internship at and accepted it, thinking it was a good move to start his career off. Seven years later and he was still there, most likely looking to make partner soon. So all in all, it definitely had been a good career decision.

Brian took a seat on the couch and Cassie offered him some coffee or water. He asked for water and she went into the refrigerator and grabbed both of them cold bottles of Voss. She came back and gave him his then sat down on the other end of the couch.

"So where's my lil' brother?" Brian was petting Sophie and looking pretty comfortable on the soft couch.

"He isn't here right now. What brings you by?" She asked to change the subject.

"Well…..I made partner," he turned to her and said with a smile.

"Oh congratulations!! That's great!" Cassidy gave him a hug and Brian chuckled a little and thanked her.

"My office took me out to celebrate and I had a few… I took a cab here… Those guys are probably still tossing back shots. I've barely eaten all day so the alcohol hit me pretty good, I guess," he said with a shrug that Sophie didn't really like.

"Yeah, it's been a long road so I'm glad it finally happened. But," he paused to yawn and stretch, causing Sophie to sit up more alert, "starting Monday I have a new case that's going to take up most of my time so I'm not sure what difference it makes anyway."

He let out a small laugh, sighed and put his head back on the head rest of the couch and closed his eyes. Cassidy was happy to notice he sounded less drunk. She didn't have the energy to deal with someone who needed taken care of at that moment.

"Well, it's all good and you should be proud of yourself. I'm sure Jamie will be, too," she said.

"Where is he anyway? It's Friday night. He should be home with his pretty wife, making a fire in the fireplace, having a glass of wine. He's probably working late," Brian said with his eyes still closed. "We text every so often cause we're both busy with work but you have to turn it off at some point." Cassidy was surprised he and Jamie stay connected as Jamie had never said anything about Brian to her.

"Well, he *may* be home. But… *this* isn't his home anymore," Cassidy said slowly, looking at Brian to see if he understood what she meant in his semi-drunken haze. He suddenly opened his eyes, slowly lifted and turned his head to her and looked very sober.

"What do you mean? I don't understand. Did you kick him out?" Brian seemed truly confused and in disbelief. Sophie didn't like this conversation anymore and jumped off the couch and ran down the hallway. Cassidy summarized the last 24 hours for Brian, including the pregnancy, and once she was finished the room fell silent. The only sounds were a few cars driving by, a dog barking in the background and the tick tock of the clock. The silence was actually comfortable.

Brian finally blew out his breath and sat closer to Cassidy. He put his arm around her, held her close, and told her how sorry he was that she was having to go through this. He added that his brother was an ass, needed his ass kicked, and apparently had no idea what he was doing. He also had a few choice descriptive words about Cindy, having met her a few times over the years.

And then he gently put his hand on her stomach and introduced himself as Uncle Brian to her unborn child. It was a very sweet gesture and brought tears to her eyes. No surprise there. This baby may have an ass for a dad but his uncle is pretty cool.

Cassidy appreciated his support and ended up being happy he stopped by, drunk and all. Brian and she always had an easy relationship so his being there didn't feel odd. But it had been a while since it was just she and he without Jamie around. It felt surprisingly comfortable and easy.

Brian was overall a sweetheart, even more that Jamie in general. Back in college, Brian was quieter and more focused whereas Jamie was often the life of the party and was usually looking for a reason to skip class. As time went on Jamie matured and started to pay more attention to school and what he would do after he graduated.

Things turned out well for Jamie especially after he and Cassie married. Brian hadn't found "the one" yet and it seemed he wasn't really looking for her either. He was happy and had a good career going but throughout the years he often showed up to various gatherings and family functions alone. There were times he had a girlfriend that would stick around for a few days or weeks or maybe even a month but that was rare. He definitely was a loner a lot of the time.

She remembered seeing Brian at a big house party in college the summer before she and Jamie were to start grad school. Brian had just finished taking the bar exam that day and had been studying for months prior. She and Jamie were on the front porch of the house where the party was being held and saw Brian walking up the driveway holding with both hands a blue cooler with a pillow laying on top. That was it. No backpack, no duffle bag, just the cooler and a pillow. It was a funny site to see. Anyone who saw him, whether they knew him or not, knew that guy was looking to have a few beers and then go to sleep somewhere.

She and Jamie had called out to him as he walked up the driveway but he hadn't seemed to hear them and walked to the back of the house. During the party they would see Brian by himself with a beer in his hand, looking like he was coming out of a daze from the months of intense studying. She remembered thinking that he seemed lonely but knew that was how he was. After all the studying he did for the bar exam he just needed to chill out and relax. Seeing him now she realized he didn't act or look much different. He still had that same smile and those dark brown eyes. And his physique was always something she noticed, from a distance of course. He still had it going on, she surprisingly thought.

"What smells so good?" Brian asked.

"Oh no, my dinner! I forgot all about it. I made extra to have for lunch tomorrow but if you want you can have it for dinner now. You said you hadn't eaten and you probably should," she said over her shoulder and she went to the kitchen to get her dinner out of the oven.

"Are you sure? I don't want to take away your meal for tomorrow. But, yeah, I do need to eat. How about if I take you up on the offer to eat the dinner and also take you to lunch tomorrow. We can go wherever you'd like and take your mind off things." He said as he got up off the couch and went into the kitchen, too.

"Thanks, Brian. Maybe I will but for now I feel really tired and just want to eat and watch some mindless TV and go to bed with a good book."

"Great, thanks, Cass. Let me help." Brian went to the cabinets and took out plates and glasses, then set the table in the formal dining room. She said they could just eat at the kitchen table or even the counter but he replied that it felt more like a celebration meal for her starting her new life, being pregnant with his future niece or nephew, and his making partner. It was a touching way to look at things, the better way to look at things, and once again she was glad he showed up.

Chapter 4

Brian left shortly after dinner but not before helping to clean up and do a few of the "manly" things around the house. He took out the garbage, replaced the light on the front porch, and brought in some cut wood from where she and Jamie kept a stack in the back yard in case she wanted to start a fire over the weekend. He had a car come for him and promised he would call to see if she wanted to go to lunch.

And sure enough he called early the next morning and they decided on a new place that was in between his downtown loft and her house in the burbs. Once again their meal was a good one with easy conversation. He told her he reached out to Jamie that morning but hadn't heard back yet. She really didn't care what Jamie said but did think Brian would let him have an earful. Brian knew to not mention the baby since Cassie hadn't told him yet. She needed to talk to Jamie about a lot of things. On a side note, she wondered how Cindy would act with Brian. Over the years Cindy would often talk about Brian being handsome and often asked if he was seeing anyone. Cassidy never understood what difference it made since Cindy was married to Bob. Poor Bob. Little did he know, little did anyone know.

After lunch Brian had to get to the office and Cassidy needed to go to the grocery store, tackle some of the things on her list and clean the house some more. The house had been a wreck because of her preparing for the meeting at the office the day before. Jamie never did any cleaning so he wasn't of much help except to make it messier. *One less thing to miss about him*, Cassidy figured.

At least some of his stuff was gone. She noticed a few of his clothes missing from his side of the closet when she was getting ready for bed. It wasn't the greatest thing to see, or not see, right before bed but this was her new reality and she had no choice but to get used to it regardless of how sad it made her.

When Cassidy was close to home, she could see Jamie's car on the street, sitting semi between her house and Cindy's. To an unknowing eye it would be hard to tell which house the car belonged to. She wondered if he did that on purpose since he had never parked on the street before. She pulled in the garage and shut the door quickly. Unloading the groceries didn't take too long since she was now making meals for one, well technically two. Once she was finished unpacking, and as if on cue, someone knocked on the front door. She opened it to see an uncomfortable looking Jamie standing there.

"Hey," he said.

"Hey," she said.

"Um, you said you wanted to talk so is this a good time?" He asked while looking down at his shoes.

"I guess so. Come on in." She let him walk past her and directed him to the dining room. It seemed less personable for the conversation they were going to have as they rarely ever sat or ate at the formal table. They each sat down and she marveled at how weird it felt to have her husband, of all people, looking like a stranger to her across the table. She decided to take the lead and get it over with.

"I'm pregnant," she said. Silence followed. A lot of silence. This being the third time she told someone about being pregnant she was starting to get a complex with all the silence that followed.

"But, Cindy is," he stupidly said.

"Yes, I know this. So am I," she said. She paused for a bit, giving Jamie a chance to say something, but he wasn't talking. He looked like a deer in headlights.

"Get your head out of your ass, Jamie" she said then sat back in her chair and exhaled. "Jamie, listen, you need to realize what you're doing and what's going on here. Maybe you need to take time to let the dust settle but you just left your wife for another woman and both of these woman are pregnant with your child. Do you understand this?"

She was so mad at him yet also felt bad for him. He truly seemed confused. But she couldn't be his friend, his confidant. That wasn't her role anymore. She didn't want to feel sympathetic towards him but it was difficult.

"Decide what needs to be done and decide quickly. Here's a first step for you. Get the rest of your shit out of my house. I noticed you took some clothes but there are a lot more things to take. I'm guessing you'll live at Cindy's house and right now I couldn't care less. We can talk about *this* house and a lot of other things at another time. Right now, I just want you out of here." She was so mad and tired of the whole situation; she just needed him to leave.

Jamie didn't say anything at first but finally mumbled an "okay" then got up and left. He said he was going to go get some boxes and be right back. She stayed at the table and let her blood pressure settle down a little bit. That was not an easy conversation. After a few moments she got up to get a glass of water and heard someone yelling in the distance and then the yelling came closer. She went to the door and Cindy was marching towards her.

"You're pregnant!? Oh that is ironic! How convenient for you! If it's even true!"

"Cindy, shut up. You two deserve each other," Cassie calmly said. Jamie came up from behind Cindy, holding two empty boxes, and told Cindy to go back in her house and that he'd be there soon. She bitched some more but then went inside.

Mr. Watkins from down the street had been walking by with his dog so Cassie knew it was only a matter of time before the whole neighborhood knew what was going on with them. Jamie finally did something smart and went about his business and started to pack things up. Cassie thought he must still have a brain in that head of his cause he knew to keep quiet. She watched him for a while and finally shook her head a little. It was really an unbelievable situation they were in. Unreal. Simply unreal.

Chapter 5

The past few weeks were a whirlwind for Cassie. She got through most of her to-do list which was a relief since most of the things she had never done before. Her new OBGYN was a wonderful woman who was also divorced and a single mom to three grown children so Cassie was comfortable when she explained her current situation.

And progress was made towards getting the divorce proceedings rolling. Her attorney was referred to her by a co-worker with the preface of his being a little nerdy but more than competent. Sure enough, Willard Oliver Jones, and that was how he introduced himself, was the pinnacle of a nerd in his mannerisms and appearance. He wore a pink bowtie, light gray suit jacket and pants and a light blue shirt. His hair was short with tight curly hair that was very blond. His voice had a slight squeak to it but the words he used required the average person to bring a thesaurus with them.

"Greetings, Cassie," Willard Oliver Jones said with a surprisingly strong handshake. "It is exceedingly enjoyable to meet you and I do express compunction for our consociate to be under these state of affairs," he said.

Cassie blink and replied, "It's nice to meet you, too." The rest of what he said she really wasn't sure of so let it go. Their meeting went off nicely and she left him confident he would do a good job. Granted, she wasn't sure of about a third of what he said in the meeting but still felt good about him being her attorney.

She felt better being in charge but was undeniably sad. She had daily moments of tears welling in her eyes and even just staring into space. Fortunately the more she did to take control the better she felt. She was handling things well but worried the stress she did feel was too much for the baby.

The same co-worker that referred Willard Oliver Jones also suggested she start to run to help handle the stress she was feeling. She used to run on the cross country team in high school and was in a competitive running club in college so was more than capable but a little worried it could hurt the baby. So she called her doctor to check and was told running would be fine until around 6 months and at that time she should switch to brisk or speed walking. This was good news to her as she recalled how good it felt to run and release the tension inside. It had been a while since she ran on a daily basis but she knew what to do to ease into it and was glad to start running again. Running always made her feel better.

During her and Jamie's marriage, Cassidy often did the yard work so knew how to run the lawn mower and other gadgets. Jamie had always wanted to hire a landscape company but she never minded the work. It was good exercise and a chance to talk with the neighbors and get some fresh air. But being pregnant slowed her down a little and she didn't want to risk doing too much just in case.

Brian was very helpful with the yard work and came over once a week to mow the lawn and do some edging. He also helped set up the nursery and put the crib and changing table together. Jamie tried to help but Cassie wanted him far away from the house. Yes, he was the father of her unborn child, but she was still pissed at him. Simple as that. He was setting up the nursery over at Cindy's so got his taste of the nursery action.

Jamie and Brian had finally talked and, as predicted, Brian gave him an earful. Brian called Cassie afterwards to tell her about the call. He didn't go into detail nor did she ask any questions about the call. Brian just wanted her to know he and Jamie did finally talk. The next time she saw Jamie he seemed visibly upset. Or maybe he was upset over something with Cindy. Cassie didn't ask him what was wrong because she didn't say much to him in general but was definitely glad Brian stepped in and said whatever it was that he said. At one point Jamie asked if she wanted to go for coffee or even lunch after one of their divorce meetings but she declined. Maybe someday they could be friends. But not that day.

Cassie still considered selling the house but since they had put down such a large down payment when they bought it the mortgage payments were not too crazy so fairly manageable for a one income family. She had never been so grateful for their making the decision to put such a hefty payment down when they first purchased the house. Both she and Jamie were good with managing money; a silver lining in what she believed was a pool of sadness. If she ever did decide to sell the house it was in good condition so no large renovations were needed. She watched HGTV enough to know. For now she decided to stay put. Plus, Willard Oliver Jones was planning to ask for the house in the divorce so he advised her to do no improvements "pending ancillary edicts." Basically "*until further notice*."

And, as predicted, the neighbors found out what happened and she was pleased to see that many rallied on her side. She appreciated their support but also, once again, felt sorry for Jamie. Even though she was mad, hurt and ever so disappointed in him, she also knew that Cindy was pushy and an ugly side of her was coming out. One that Cassie had seen throughout the years but never really mentioned to Jamie. All Jamie had seen was a hot looking next door neighbor but now he was really getting to know a different side to Cindy. Based on the way Jamie looked when Cassie saw him at divorce appointments or just outside in the yard sometimes she truly felt he wasn't 100% happy with Cindy. His life was changing in many unexpected ways.

Chapter 6

Brian turned out to be a life saver in many ways. Not only did he help Cassie do things around the house and help set up the nursery but he had also been a shoulder to cry on in the early days, which Cassie had done often. Brian listened more than he offered any advice which was fine with her. She just wanted to vent. She would have turned to Joe but he was busy with Jack. While they did talk at work and an occasional lunch here and there she didn't want to bring Joe down. At the time he was in the beginning stages of a relationship where everything was good; the overplayed song on the radio (Oh, this song is great once you really listen to the words!), the long line in a grocery store (The magazines are so fun to flip through!) or even a traffic jam (It's so nice to open the windows and feel the air!). The last thing Cassie wanted to do was throw her balloon popping situation into his pot of happiness.

Some of her good friends had reached out to ask how she was doing but she kept it upbeat and brief. Cassie just didn't want to depress anyone else because of Jamie's infidelity. And she didn't want to be the one people avoided talking to either. So Brian had been the lucky one. He really didn't seem to mind and she had been truly grateful. Over those first few weeks to months after Jamie left she and Brian had developed a nice friendship and she was thankful he was in her life.

Aside from Brian coming by the house to help her with general maintenance or take her to dinner they had also enjoyed going on walks around the neighborhood or the nearby park. One weekend they went antiques shopping which neither of them had ever done but somehow they had found themselves in a charming little town about 30 miles outside of the city limits. They walked around the cute area with its quaint shops and very polite townspeople. Many of the polite people asked when Cassie was due and would make comments about how happy she and Brian were, presuming him to be the baby's father.

Neither Cassie nor Brian corrected anyone either because they didn't want to seem rude. And maybe they both liked to appear to be a happy and *in love* family. They never talked about it together and just let people assume, no harm done.

And during a typical work week many times they'd find themselves having lengthy and late night phone calls which both seemed to hate ending but both had early mornings, too. Cassie really appreciated his companionship and missed him being around. He had come by as much as he could when Jamie first moved out but now, many months later, he wasn't able to visit as much as he did because he was extra busy at work since he had made partner.

He also had started to, surprisingly, date someone so his time was pretty well taken. Cassie didn't know when he had time to meet anyone but was happy for him. She understood he had his own life to live yet found herself missing him and the friendship they formed without Jamie in the mix.

At the same time she knew it was only a friendship and that it couldn't progress to anything more than that. She wasn't sure she would even want to do anything to jeopardize their relationship. But that thought did pop in her head from time to time. She wasn't sure what that meant but chalked it up to being hormonal and alone.

Around halfway through the pregnancy Cassie's work was pretty busy which helped her keep busy. Her mind didn't stray too much when she was in the office so she was productive. The company was doing so well that they hired a few new people, one being a VP of Business Development. His name was Keith Jensen and he knew the market well. He had an impressive resume of sales development and market analysis in their industry and Cassie's boss was really happy to have him on board.

Keith was not only new to the company but to the area as well since he had to relocate there. He had a lot of people in the office take him out for dinner and drinks on many occasions and some even showed him around the area on weekends. Granted, most of these people were the women in the office. It didn't hurt that Keith was very attractive, and single, so his social card was often full.

The ladies were very pretty happy he was hired. Cassie didn't partake in the social side of work mainly because she was pregnant but she did notice that Keith impressively worked long hours and traveled a good portion of the week so while he did like to be social he also liked to stay in and, she heard from some co-workers, read and play the piano. Yes, he was dreamy. He was definitely a fun distraction to Cassie at times.

A new project had come along and since Cassie were the Senior Project Manager she had consulted directly with Keith on a few ideas to get his input. For a few weeks she and her team, as well Keith, had worked long hours so they grew to know each other well. He was an interesting man, told good stories, was funny, smart, and a good listener. He was truly interested in her pregnancy, even surprising her with a baby proofing kit and coming to her house to set it all up for the baby. And he brought a present to the Baby Shower her office lady friends had. She found herself looking forward to seeing him at work and sometimes she thought he was happy to see her, too.

Time was definitely going by. Cassie saw Jamie all too often since he was her next door neighbor. Sometimes she felt like she saw him more than when they were married. Too many times she saw Cindy and her growing belly. Cassie had her own expanding stomach and found herself at times feeling a bit nostalgic for the friendship she and Cindy had. If things were different, way different, and they were both pregnant they could have really enjoyed this time together. Cassie had friends from college she talked to on a regular basis but most were far away so a quick visit wasn't an easy option, either.

Jamie's mom, Pepper, was very sweet and stopped by every so often. She never overstayed her visit and Cassie appreciated the time they had together. Pepper was disappointed that Jamie did what he did but she also let it be their issue to work out and provided a shoulder to lean on. During one visit Cassie got the impression that Pepper wasn't very fond of Cindy but she would never say that out loud. The situation wasn't an easy one to deal with and they were all adjusting however they could.

Likewise she missed Joe and their crazy conversations but, again, he was busy with his own things. Hanging out with Keith would be nice, and he asked her often enough, but she didn't want to start a relationship, plutonic or not, with a male co-worker, especially when her life was going to change extensively once she had the baby.

Cassie definitely felt lonely at times but when the baby kicked it warmed her heart. She and the baby would be okay, she had no doubt, and she was excited to meet him or her. She could have found out the sex of the baby but wanted to be surprised. Jamie and Cindy found out they were having a girl. She wasn't sure what that bit of information meant to her but she did feel bothered. Maybe because she imagined Jamie and Cindy during the ultrasound all lovey and excited to find out what they were having.

While Cassie was alone at her doctor appointments. Granted, that was by choice because Joe, Brian, her parents and Jamie's parents all offered to go with her but she never took them up on their offers. She wanted her husband there but sadly that didn't feel right either. So she chose to go solo.

Chapter 7

Cassie's due date was coming up. And so was Cindy's. She could see Jamie freaking out and hoped he was holding his job down well since he was about to have two children. Cassidy's anger towards Jamie had simmered down over the past few months mainly because she saw how miserable he seemed.

The times she saw Cindy outside she looked distracted and cranky. And the times she saw both Cindy and Jamie, they looked nothing like a loving couple about to have a baby. Jamie's situation was all because of his choices, Cassie knew this, but it was still hard to see him so unhappy. According to Willard Oliver Jones her and Jamie's divorce was close to final so maybe that would be a load off of Jamie's mind.

Cass planned to take off three months maternity leave so had a lot of things to finish at work before she left. She was delegating things and relying on many co-workers to help keep things running smoothly while she was out. Even though she would be a phone call away if someone needed something, she knew they wouldn't want to bother her, which she would appreciate, so wanted as much done as possible to enjoy this special time with the baby.

One night Cassie came home tired and hungry and looking forward to a big dinner and flip through the channels on TV. When she pulled in her driveway she saw Brian's car on the street and he and Jamie talking outside. She went in the house, fed Sophia, changed into her comfy pjs and put her premade dinner in the oven. Looking outside she saw Brian alone in Cindy's driveway rubbing the back of his neck and looking perplexed. Jamie returned with a duffle bag and Brian watched as he loaded the car. Is Jamie leaving Cindy?

Then no sooner had that thought entered her mind did she hear Cindy's voice crying out. What was going on? Both Jamie and Brian went to her and helped her in the car. *She's in labor*, thought Cassidy. The moment was surreal for her. During the past few months she knew Jamie was technically no longer hers but seeing Cindy in labor, about to give birth to Jamie's baby girl, made it all too real. She felt sad, simple as that. From her vantage point she wasn't sure if they could see her watching but she didn't care. Jamie looked her way for a moment and Cassie held her breath. It was a moment she may never forget. He then got in the car, backed out, and drove off to the hospital to begin a life with his new family.

Chapter 8

"It's a nice, sunny day for a one year old birthday party," cooed Cassidy. As she held her baby in her arms she reflected on the past year or so. So much had happened it was unreal to think about. One minute she is semi-happily married and wanting a child and the next she is divorced and pregnant.

Today she has a wonderful one year old baby boy and her ex-husband and HIS little 13 month old baby girl are living next door with her EX best friend. And her semi-new boyfriend (that word "boyfriend" made it sound like she was 12) was coming over soon to help her set up for the birthday party. Incredible how life can change so suddenly.

Cassidy shakes her head at the wonder of it all and snaps back to the present. She lays her baby down for his morning nap, stares at him for a while, puts the baby monitor on and heads downstairs to finish her list of things to do for the party. Keith (yep, Keith) would be over soon and she wanted to have a glass of wine with him first, to settle her nerves over the hodgepodge list of guests expected at the party.

She had invited Jamie and his bitch of a fiancé, Cindy, Brian and his girlfriend of a few months whom she met a few times, Jamie's parents, her parents, Joe and his boyfriend, Jack, some co-workers from the office and a few neighbors, too. She opted for a 2 pm party for a few reasons. The first was that Bailey was happiest and least fussy around that time so she figured that could make the party more enjoyable for all around. She didn't want to have one too late as the guest of honor may turn cranky closer to his bedtime.

And she also didn't want anyone to drink too much wine or whatever she had to offer so maybe an afternoon one year old birthday party would keep everyone in check and under control. The crowd of guests was unique with a host of personalities and the last thing she wanted to remember for her baby's first birthday was Cindy getting drunk and making a scene (it happened!) or any of the co-workers hitting on Keith (it happened!).

Cassidy was working on the food she would serve when she heard a knock on the door. She opened it to find Cindy standing there. Blah. Where was that glass of wine she wanted to drink?

"Hey," said Cindy.

"Um, hi?" Cassie said with a questioning and sprinkle of bitch tone.

"Listen, I just wanted to come over ahead of everyone and talk to you privately." Cindy seemed uncomfortable. This should be interesting.

"Okay," Cassie said slowly.

"Well, I wanted to say," she paused to inhale then in a rush said, "that I hope you don't plan on embarrassing yourself and hitting on Jamie today. I just want to let Lilly enjoy time with her brother on his birthday," Cindy said in practically one breath.

What the hell is this all about, Cassie wondered. And since when did Cindy care if Lilly and Bailey spent time together?

"What are you talking about, Cindy? I don't 'hit' on Jamie. I don't even know if I hit on him when I met him in college. What are you talking about?"

"I see the way you look at him and it makes me uncomfortable. It makes him uncomfortable, too. He told me! And you have to accept that he and I are together now and have a family. Sure, he has his son over here and stuff, whatever, but I can accept that."

Cassidy was getting pissed. It is one thing to say she "hits" on Jamie, when she simply doesn't, but to act as if Bailey is "over here and stuff" is poking the mama bear.

"Cindy, I appreciate your coming over here. I really do cause, once again, it reminds me of what a pain in the ass you are because sometimes, surprisingly, I feel bad for you and all that you have going on."

Cindy starts to talk and Cassie puts her hand up to stop her and continues. "Listen to me. I do not hit on Jamie. I do not want to hit on Jamie. I have no interest in Jamie except as Bailey's father and to make sure they spend time together, which he wants to do on his own anyway whether you want to accept that or not. I am actually impressed with how Jamie is juggling two small children in different homes and trying his best to be a good dad to both. It's all about the children. Not me. Not you." Cassie pointed her finger at Cindy.

"Now listen carefully…..do not come over here and act like my son is an inconvenience that you have to *deal* with. He, along with Lilly, are innocent babies brought into an exceptional family situation. If you reference that Bailey is 'over here and stuff' again I promise you I will kick your ass all the way across MY yard back to YOUR yard and then once more just because I'm sure I'll like it. I have never been more serious." She was pissed.

Cindy started to say something defensive but saw the look in Cassidy's eyes and surprisingly knew better. Both stood there and looked at each other for a few moments, with Cindy finally turning her sorry ass away and walking back to her house. Cassie watched her until she was gone and shut the door quietly. She couldn't believe how delusional Cindy was. It was concerning to her for Lilly's sake. She would definitely let Jamie know about this conversation and went looking for that damn wine.

Chapter 9

Bailey's first birthday party was a success. Everyone was on their best behavior and seemed to have a really nice time. Keith had come over early as promised and was a huge help. Cassidy kept the party to just a few hours for obvious reasons and when time was up, no one was really trying to get out the door too fast nor, shockingly, was Cassie trying to get anyone to leave. Even Cindy seemed to be not so annoying. The wind was out of Cindy's sails for now because of the conversation she and Cassie had. She would be annoying again. No worries there. But Cass was glad today was a good day for Bailey.

The only thing that seemed a little off was Brian and his girlfriend, Jane. While Cassie had seen them together here and there over the past few months Brian never seemed to look, or act, completely happy. Jane was visibly smitten with Brian and always hanging on his arm, sitting next to him, looking dreamily into his eyes, but Brian never seemed to notice. He was always a gentleman with her, offering to get her another glass of whatever, giving her his jacket when she was cold and things like that. It just seemed that something wasn't quite right on his side.

Maybe he was stressed from work and just had a lot on his mind. Cassie would reach out to him in a few days and see if he was okay. He had helped her so much when her life was in a shambles and as much as he could up until even the last few months, probably annoying Jane some with the small amount of time he did spend at Cassie's house, but definitely a help to Cassie. The least she could do was reach out and see how he was doing.

Keith helped her clean up while Cassie got Bailey to bed. Bailey was very tired and went to sleep easily while Cassie stayed there and stared at him and rubbed his back softly. Having a baby was so surreal. She had never felt such love for another being as she did for Bailey. When he smiled or laughed, her heart melted.

Going back to work after her maternity leave ended may have been the most difficult thing she had ever done. Thank God her neighbor, Della, offered to watch Bailey a few days a week while she was at work. And Jamie's mom watched both her grandchildren the other days of the week with Cassie's parents as backup but they lived farther away. While it was hard to go back, she was glad Bailey was still at home safe and sound.

Chapter 10

The next day Bailey slept in a little so Cassie was able to get up and have some coffee and read the Sunday paper. She hadn't done that in ages it seemed. Keith had left the night before as he had to pack and take a mid-morning flight for an all week conference that started early Monday. She didn't mind the solitude and put her face to the sun, closing her eyes and listening to the birds chirping and other neighborhood sounds. The baby monitor was on low but she could still hear the soft snores from Bailey, happy he was getting a good sleep from his busy birthday party.

She was just about to get up and grab another cup of coffee when she saw Brian walking into the backyard. He was casually dressed in khaki cargo shorts, a Brown University t-shirt and flip flops. Even though she was surprised to see him there she still took a moment to admire his physique as he walked towards her. She wasn't sure why she was checking him out and found herself literally looking him up and down. And she realized neither of them had spoken and they sort of looked at each other for a beat or two. Finally she asked what he was doing there so early in the morning.

"I was up early cause I had to turn in a brief for a client by 6 am this morning, and once that was done I went for a drive. I had a feeling you would be out here enjoying the morning. It's so nice out," he looked around the yard and up at the sky. "So I took a chance and came over and walked back here. I was right," he smiled at her and oddly touched her arm for a moment then just as quickly moved his hand back to his side. "Is, um, Bailey still sleeping?" He cleared his throat seemingly embarrassed with the brief show of affection. So was Cassie.

"Yeah, he was pretty tired from the party. He got up earlier and had a bottle then went back to sleep. I'm enjoying the quiet. It's nice to be out here without any neighbors up yet," she smiled and nodded her head towards Cindy's house. "I was just about to get another cup of coffee. Would you like one? Maybe some breakfast? I can make eggs and bacon."

"Oh, yeah, thanks," he said excitedly. "I can get it for you though so sit tight. I also brought some bagels and cream cheese from that deli you like around the corner. I'll go back to my car and get them and meet you back here in a few."

"Oh, um, okay," sputtered Cass. He barely heard her as he did a little jog back to his car for the bagels. She checked him out again. What was her deal?

How strange for him to be here so early, she thought as she went back to her chair. And with a mix of emotion she was secretly glad that Keith wasn't there. Huh, wonder why. Brian came back a few moments later with two cups of coffee, two glasses of orange juice, the delicious bagels, cream cheese, a spreading knife, napkins and a folded letter all on a tray. He placed the tray on the table and sat in a chair next to her.

"Thanks, Brian, this is perfect. I can't believe how great your timing is, I was just getting hungry and wasn't sure what to make. I love these bagels!" She went to the tray, picked up a bagel and spread the cream cheese on it and took a bite. She was almost embarrassed with her show of hunger but those bagels were her favorite. Brian smiled and knew she was happy he stopped by.

"You're welcome and no problem. I'm just glad you were up and home, I was hoping to get a chance to talk to you one on one."

"Oh, okay, why? What's up?" She reached for a napkin to wipe cream cheese from her greedy mouth and sat back down.

Brian prepared a bagel too and both sat in silence eating them while looking out at the yard. It was a nice yard that backed up into a large horse farm. It was nice to know a housing development or any such building would most likely not be built there to obstruct the view. Her yard faced west so the sunsets were spectacular.

Once they finished the bagels Brian took the letter he had on the tray and handed it to Cassie. She looked at him questioningly then read it once, then twice, then looked at him in surprise. "Congratulations, Brian! This is great! What a huge promotion!"

"Thanks. It really took me by surprise. I knew my boss was happy with my work, my billable hours and a few new group projects he had me manage, but I had no idea this was up his sleeve. I'm happy about it but to be honest not sure if I want to really up and move that far away. I mean London would be a great place to live, and I sort of always wanted to visit there, but to live there indefinitely, or at least until the new office is up and running…..I'm just not sure. I don't need to give my answer for a few days so I wanted to talk it out with you and see what you think."

"Oh, well, like I said I'm happy for you, if this is what you want," Cassie said as she looked over the letter again. "It sounds like a once in a lifetime opportunity but

I understand your being unsure. But, then again, what are you unsure about exactly?"

"Well, to be honest," he said slowly, "it's more of a personal thing."

Brian didn't talk for a while. Cassie realized she was holding her breath to hear what he had to say. But he wasn't saying anything.

"Do you mean Jane?" She finally asked. She was sure that's what his personal thing was and she actually felt a little jealous and had no reason to feel that way. "You two have been going out for a while so I get why you wouldn't want to leave. I was actually going to call you today and ask how you two were doing."

"You were? Why?"

"Well, last night at the party, and even a few other times, you two seemed a bit off. Well, you mostly. But then again you're at the office a lot and traveling, too, so I'm probably just reading it all wrong."

"No, you're right," he said with his voice trailing off. Once again he wasn't saying anything, this time staring at the sky. Cassie wanted to push this conversation along to try and help him work through his decision but he seemed at a loss for words.

"So do you think it's a bad idea to take this job and leave what you and Jane have? Or do you want to ask her to go with you and see how your relationship does?"

"No," Brian replied rather quickly. "To be honest, she hasn't been a factor in my deciding what to do. I mean I just got this letter on Friday but I haven't even told her about it or even thought about what she'll think," he threw his head back with an exhale and then forward into his hands with a groan. "Wow, now I feel horrible!"

Brian leaned forward and hung his head in his hands for a bit. Cassie just kept quiet and let him digest all that he was saying and realizing. She was confused and wondering what his personal reason was for maybe not taking the job but didn't want to push too much. She sipped her coffee and eyed the bagels, but didn't want to be rude and eat while his life was at a cross roads. As if reading her mind, Brian lifted his head, shook it a little, and then said, "Let's eat another bagel!"

So, as simple as that, they changed the subject and enjoyed the bagels and coffee. They talked some more about the party the night before and how happy Joe was and what a great guy Jack seemed to be. Brian had met Joe over the years and liked him a lot. The feelings were mutual but add a little lust to Joe's feelings for Brian and you're all caught up.

She heard Bailey stirring on the monitor and was about to go get him when Brian said he'd love to get his nephew. She reminded him he would need his diaper changed but that didn't faze Uncle Brian. He was really good with both his niece and nephew. If he went to London he would miss out on a lot. She figured that was a factor on his mind, too.

As he went in to get Bailey, Cassie realized that Brian never really said what his personal reasons were for not leaving. It didn't seem like Jane was on his mind with this decision but she wondered what was. Or maybe missing Bailey and Lilly is what he was referring to for his "personal" reason. That made total sense.

She eventually heard Brian on the baby monitor say hi to Bailey and could hear Bailey cooing and talking his cute baby talk back. They were so cute together. She would miss seeing them spend time with each other if he went to London. He really loved the babies and they loved him, too.

"Hey, Bailey, my main man! Did you have a nice birthday party?" Cassie heard Brian on the baby monitor. "Mommy said you were tired and that you'd have a wet diaper. Let's see what we've got here." Cassie could hear the unsnapping of Bailey's pajamas. "Yep, that's a wet one. Okay, let's get this done and go outside, it's nice and warm out and Mommy is waiting for us."

She wondered if Brian remembered the monitor was on while he talked his baby talk to Bailey. It was really cute. Especially with Brian being such a manly man. She found herself smiling. Wow, why was she reacting this way to Brian all of a sudden?

"So, Bailey, guess what?" Cassie could hear Brian getting a new diaper from the shelf below the changing table and opening the box of wipes next to them. "My boss wants me to move to London… London is really far away but a pretty cool place… I don't know what to do… I would miss seeing you and your sister growing up…" There were continual sounds of Bailey making noises as if he were agreeing with him. "And… I'd miss your mom… A lot… I don't know what to do, have any advice?" Bailey started to make his "ba ba ba" noise, which meant he wanted his bottle. "Yeah, yeah, you want your bottle. Okay, one more snap on your pajamas and… Okay, let's go, Little Man."

Okay, did Brian just say he'd miss her… a lot? Cassie was shocked. Did he mean yeah, no big, sure I'll miss her or did he mean something more? And did he want her to know this? Was he trying to tell her this earlier? She quickly turned off the monitor and started to read the paper again, acting as if she heard nothing. She didn't know if he realized the monitor was on and didn't want to embarrass him, or her!

He and Bailey came outside a few moments later. Bailey smiled ear to ear when he saw Cassie and she did the same to him. She reached for him and snuggled him on her lap while he had his bottle. He had been able to hold it on his own for a long time now and this little bit of independence made her kind of sad. He was growing up too fast. Brian would definitely miss little milestones like this. But he also needed to have his own life, get married, and have his own kids. She decided then that she wouldn't bring up his missing Bailey and Lilly "growing up" because he had enough to figure out.

She slightly turned to Brian and out of the corner of her eye saw him looking at the monitor. He could see the light was off so knew it wasn't on. He had a look on his face she couldn't quite recognized but she figured that he was probably wondering when the monitor got turned off. She didn't say anything and reached for her orange juice with her free hand and let the moment pass. After a few moments, so did Brian.

Chapter 11

Brian and Cassie never finished their conversation about his moving to London. Soon after he had brought Bailey down that early morning Jamie and Lilly came over after seeing Brian's car on the street. Jamie looked surprised to see the tray of food and drink on the table but still helped himself to a bagel. The moment had definitely passed for Cassie to talk to Brian again about London. Although she wondered if she and Brian needed to have a conversation about what he said to Bailey. But did she really want to open that can of worms? She knew she felt attracted to Brian at times. Just about anyone was attracted to Brian. He had a look about that was strong. He wasn't a "pretty boy" nor did he look like a GQ model. Brian was just handsome and quiet. It was a nice mix.

As many times as Cassie caught herself checking him out throughout the years she was so used to never letting it go past the precious line of friendship that it seemed beyond crazy to consider Brian more than a friend. But she knew he was a great guy and they had grown very close over the past year or two. Cassie was well aware that she would have had a hard time dealing with all the changes of Jamie moving out, being pregnant, reorganizing finances and so much more had it not been for Brian. He was a shoulder to cry on, an ear to vent her emotions to, and a friend to be with when she felt lonely.

During her pregnancy Brian would often come over for a surprise visit and bring a food that she had recently been craving. One night they talked on the phone for about an hour and it was close to midnight when they hung up. She had told Brian during the conversation that she was craving b-b-q flavored chips with ranch salad dressing and needed to hang up the phone and get to bed before she drove herself to the supermarket. They hung up and she went upstairs to wash her face and get ready for bed. After a while she heard her phone ping that she had a text. It was from Brian telling her to go look on her front porch. She did and there was a bag of b-b-q chips, a bottle of ranch dressing and her favorite candy bar. He was nowhere to be found. She gathered the snacks smiling the whole time. He really was a great guy.

Late that day and into the next week Cassie found herself wondering many times if Brian would take the job in London. She, herself, had mixed emotions about his moving and that confused her, too. It took effort but she snapped herself out of her racing mind and tried to not think about Brian, it seemed like her thoughts were getting out of control and she knew she had to get a grip. If he did move to London, she would miss him and Bailey would be denied time with his uncle and that wasn't something she wanted to happen. But, the bottom line was, it wasn't her decision.

Jamie, fortunately, spent a lot of time with Bailey. He had been doing a good job splitting his time between the two children and also doing things with all three of them together and without Cindy. It wasn't as weird to see him and Lilly together as it had been in the beginning. She didn't like when Cindy came over with Jamie, as she did from time to time, but only because Cindy was annoying. She whined, complained and ignored Bailey often. The whole dynamic was weird for lack of a better word but Cassie tried not to dwell on it and was happy that Jamie spent time with his son.

Cassie had been busy that week with new projects at work and making sure she spent quality time with Bailey when she came home. The week went by fast and before she had a chance to miss him, Keith was back. He came into her office midday on that Friday, having just flown in that morning. He had his carry-on bag thrown over his shoulder, his briefcase in one hand and a beautiful bouquet of flowers in the other. Cassie was always amazed at how light Keith could pack for an all week trip. *One of the many wonders of Keith*, she thought. He was smart, funny, confident, talented and very romantic. She was a lucky girl.

"How's my favorite lady today?" He handed her the flowers and kissed her softly yet fully on the lips. He tasted like cinnamon and downright delicious. She missed him more than she realized. Work had been so busy and her evenings had been a whirlwind so she didn't have a lot of time to even miss him but now she was glad he was back.

"Oooh, you taste good. And thank you for the flowers!"

"My pleasure, pretty lady. So, how's it going? How's Bailey?"

"He's great. All is good at home and here at the office. I'm glad you're back. I missed you…." She lifted her head to kiss him again and he obliged. They barely kissed at the office because they wanted to keep things professional but at that moment she didn't care. Nor did he seem to and after a few moments they broke apart and chuckled a little, both sort of embarrassed at their show of affection.

"Well, I've got a meeting and need to grab a quick sandwich. Do you want to order in tonight and watch a movie with Bailey? Maybe Finding Nemo?" He asked her with a sparkle in his eye. Cassie laughed cause she wasn't sure who liked that movie more, Bailey or Keith.

"Sounds great! I'm so glad it's Friday," she said.

"Me, too. Order the food around 6 and I'll pick it up on my way over. Should be there by 7." He kissed her again, a quick one this time, and off he went.

She watched him walk out and also watched one of the receptionists say hi to him with an exaggerated wave, another touched his arm for some reason and said something to him then laughed at her own comment, while flipping her hair no less, and another just stared as he walked by.

Keith was serious eye candy in the office, had been since his first day, and Cassie found herself more than once happy that they had gotten together. Their relationship started slow and turned into a really nice friendship. Because she was pregnant with Bailey she had no interest in a new relationship, especially since she had still been heartbroken over Jamie and their splitting up. Keith seemed to understand her feelings and never pressured her into more than friends. He seemed to know that she needed to let things settle down from the breakup of her marriage and also to prepare herself for motherhood.

After Bailey was born and she became accustomed to having a newborn she started to get more feelings for Keith. She liked him being around, liked how he was with Bailey, and liked him as a person overall. Next thing you know, they became more than friends. She was glad he waited for her to come around. And a bonus was that Cindy openly flirted with Keith when she saw him at Cassie's house and Keith was polite yet barely talked to her. Truth be told, it made Cassie happy when she watched Cindy make a fool of herself. She deserved that much.

Chapter 12

That night, before Keith came over, Brian called Cassie and told her he was taking the job in London. She was surely happy for him but also a little sad, too. His boss said he could go over until the new office was situated and running efficiently and play it by ear after that. So it wasn't an all or nothing deal and he could see how it went.

Even though Cassie didn't help him sort out his thoughts that morning he came by with the bagels she figured since the transfer to London wasn't as long as he initially thought maybe he felt it was a good opportunity after all. She was happy for him. He also told Cassie that Jane wasn't thrilled about it but they were going to keep their relationship going and try it long distance. Her work in the fashion industry had her traveling often to Paris so she planned to hop over to London when she could. Cassie wanted Brian to be happy and whether it was with Jane or not was yet to be determined.

During the call he asked if he could take her and Bailey to dinner before he left which was in a few weeks. She said yes and that she would get a sitter. The dinner would be more relaxing without the baby there and she wanted that especially since he was leaving the country for a long time. They agreed on a day and he said he'd call with final plans. She hung up and realized she had a smile of her face. Interesting…

After talking with Brian she felt bummed out and almost called Keith to cancel but knew he had been looking forward to their date. Keith showed up as planned and they ate dinner while watching the movie with Bailey. When the video was over Cassie gave Bailey a bath and read him a few books while he dozed in her arms. She sat there with him softly snoring and thought about Brian, again. His decision to leave had really hit her hard. They had their friendship but truth be told they hadn't hung out together in a while. They were both busy with work and their relationships with Jane and Keith and of course there was Bailey. There were phone calls and texts to touch base periodically but not like it had been. She realized she missed him.

After a little longer Cassie sighed and put Bailey down in his crib and covered him up, feeling blessed for such moments. She turned on the monitor and came downstairs to find Keith in the living room with a fire in the fireplace, a new bottle of wine opened and soft music playing in the background. Typical Keith.

Keith handed her a glass of wine and they sat on the floor, leaning into each other with their backs on the sofa. Both were silent as they watched the flames dance around, listening to the soft crackles of the fire. After what seemed a long time, Keith turned to Cassie and looked her in the eyes. He kept his eyes on hers while he slowly leaned in to kiss her. Their kiss turned passionate and went on for a while.

When they came up for air, Keith softly said, "I love you, Cassie." It was the first time either of them had said the "L" word. She wasn't too surprised to hear him say it but was more surprised that she didn't immediately say it back to him.

Realizing she had been taking too long to respond she finally replied that she loved him, too. And she did. Right? Yes, she did. He almost exhaled when she finally said it. She did feel a strong emotion towards him and was definitely attracted to him. She figured her delay in answering him had to do with the fact that the only person she had ever been in true love with was Jamie. She had some boyfriends in high school and in college before she met Jamie, but none that she would say she had been in love with. It wasn't an emotion that came to her easy.

Keith was a great catch for any woman and as much as she had missed him the past week and knew he was a wonderful man, there was definitely something missing. She wished she felt head over heels, crazy in love with him but the most she felt was that she liked him a whole lot and wanted him around. But was it love? She didn't know for sure and knew it wasn't the time to bring up her uncertainties so she went with the moment and they enjoyed the rest of the evening.

Chapter 13

The next morning over breakfast, while feeding Bailey his jar of bananas, torn up pieces of toast and bowl of rice, Cassie casually mentioned to Keith that Brian was moving to England. She added, albeit casually, that he wanted to take her out to dinner before he left. Keith didn't reply right away and the silence got a little uncomfortable.

"Um, Keith, did you hear me?" Cassie asked as she was wiping Bailey's face.

"Yeah, sorry. That's great for Brian. He must be doing well at his company for that sort of a promotion. How long will he be there for?" He suddenly got up from the table and started to busy himself with making a cup of coffee and pouring cereal in a bowl. His back was towards her the whole time.

"Well, I don't know the details yet but so far it sounds like his boss said he needs to stay there until the new office is up and running which could take months to maybe a year but again I'm not sure of the specifics," Cassie replied.

"Uh huh. So will he come back then? Back to the U.S.? After the office is set up?" Keith sounded like he was trying to figure out a mystery. Cassie was getting a little annoyed.

"I doubt he knows that yet but again I don't know the details. I would be surprised if he moved there forever instead of just for a few months or even the year." Cassie wanted him to turn around and look at her but he was staring out of the window over the kitchen sink holding his bowl of cereal and spoon in front of him. She wondered why he was acting so weird all of a sudden.

"What about Jane?" He asked as he snapped out of his daze.

"This I do know. Brian said they're going to try to keep the relationship going and see each other when they can. But it'll probably be her going to see him more so since she's overseas fairly often because of her job. I'm sure I'll get more info when he and I go to dinner," said Cassie.

"Probably. Yeah. Well, I hope it works out for them," Keith said with a flair of determination.

"Me, too," said Cassie. But something inside of her wasn't believing that.

Later that evening, after Keith had left and Cassie put Bailey down for bed, Brian called her. She was surprised to hear from him knowing there had to be a lot to do before his move and figured he and Jane were spending as much time together as they could. But at the same time she was really happy to hear from him.

"Hey, Cass, how's it going?" Brian asked cheerfully.

"Hi Brian! It's good. I just got Bailey down and was about to pour myself a glass of wine and relax a little. How're you doing? Getting all packed up for London?" Cassie cradled the phone while pouring her wine and cutting up some cheese for a little snack. Her neck started to hurt so she put the phone on the counter and hit the speaker button.

"Ha!" Brian's voice echoed through the kitchen. "I did some packing but my firm has a moving company that will come in and basically pack everything up for me. I don't need to do a thing if I don't want to. But I don't really want some big mover dude folding up my underwear so I plan to pack up most of my clothes on my own," he laughed.

"Yeah, I would, too!" She told Brian to hold on and picked up her wine and plate of cheese and crackers and brought them out to the back patio. She came back in for the baby monitor, phone and a lighter. Now she was ready to unwind.

"Okay, sorry about that. I didn't have enough hands to bring everything out on the back patio. It's such a nice night out I wanted to enjoy it and relax a little," Cassie told Brian. She had just mowed her lawn and planted some new flowers that day so things looked really nice. She had put up Tiki Torches too and lit one up with the lighter. And she also took Brian off speaker phone incase Cindy was lurking in the bushes.

"Oh, I didn't mean to interrupt any of your down time. We can talk more when we go to dinner," Brian said.

"No!" Cassie practically yelled. Well, she kind of did yell. "Oh, sorry, I didn't mean to be so loud," she laughed nervously. "I'm actually glad you called. I was going to at least text you tonight to see how things were going. I didn't want to call and bother you while you were packing or whatever. So I'm really glad you called." *Wow, stop saying you're glad he called*, she thought.

"Oh, good, I'm glad, too," Brian said and Cassie could tell he was smiling. They were like two idiots with big smiles on their faces. She was holding the phone to her ear tight and could hear him pouring something to drink.

"I'm going to join you in a drink," he said. "I wish I was there with you though."

Cassie's stomach did a little flip when she heard what he said. She didn't know what to say back but didn't want to make him feel embarrassed by not saying anything. She needed to come up with something clever to say that had a hint of flirty with it yet a hint of no big deal…fast!

"Um, what are you drinking?" She asked. *Yeah, real flirty.*

Brian replied a beat later, "Oh, I found some gin in the freezer so I'm having gin and soda on the rocks. I know it's a work night and I need to get up early but I deserve a good drink." She hears him take a sip. "It's actually really good."

"I'm sure it's been a long week for you. So, what else is going on? Are you excited for London? Will you know anyone there?" They went on talking for close to two hours. She refilled her wine glass a few times and could hear him freshening his drink, too. They talked about London, Bailey and Lilly, Jamie and Cindy, her work, his work, the weather and just about everything under the sun except for Keith and Jane. And she was fine with that.

She was thoroughly enjoying the conversation and wished more than once that he was there on the back patio, too. Their call reminded her of how much she enjoyed his company. She missed their friendship. Back in the day they would talk about so many random topics no matter where they were; on the back patio, out to dinner, while running errands for baby things, wherever. He was around often and especially during the weekends but once Keith and Jane were in the picture, their "friendship" wasn't what it had been initially.

Maybe they both knew that there was a limit or even expiration date to their relationship because of Jamie. So when Jane and Keith arrived to the scene they let things fizzle out. Maybe their friendship would have gone to another level. She definitely found him attractive and thought he felt the same but then again she had been pregnant at the time so her hormones were out of whack. She had a feeling that if he were there on the patio instead of being on the phone something may have happen between them. Or maybe she just needed to get some sleep. Brian and she were friends, that was for certain, and he was moving to another continent, another certainty. So all in all, this call from him was probably just a way to have a nice chat with her before he left. Nothing more. She wasn't sure how that made her feel but went with it anyway.

"Well, it's getting late and I need to get some sleep. And so do you," she said with a yawn. "I'm really glad you called. I've missed these long conversations."

"Yeah, so have I, Cass," Brian said softly. Almost sadly.

Neither spoke for a few moments until Cassie heard Bailey on the monitor starting to stir. She wanted to get all her things back in the house and lock up, get Bailey a sippy cup of water and go upstairs before he started to get too worked up.

"Well, let me know when we're going to dinner. I'm looking forward to it!" She tried to sound more upbeat versus almost sad like Brian had suddenly sounded but wasn't sure if she was pulling it off.

"Me, too. I'll get back to you on dinner. I'll talk to you soon, Cass," Brian said.

"Okay, thanks for calling. Good night." She hung up before either of them said anything more, or less.

A few nights later Keith surprised Cassie with babysitting arrangements and dinner out on the town. Her parents picked Bailey up after she got home from work and wanted to keep him for the night. She rarely asked her parents for help with Bailey knowing they had enough on their social calendar, so was happy for them and Bailey to have a night together. Keith had dinner reservations at her favorite restaurant, The Martini, at 7:30. And then he had another surprise planned for afterward. It was the middle of the week and she and Keith rarely did anything on a work night. Cassie checked the calendar quickly wondering if there was an anniversary or birthday she was missing, but it just seemed to be an ordinary day.

Keith showed up looking dapper in a suit she hadn't seen before. She was glad to have worn her little black dress even though it was just an ordinary week day. He looked at her appraisingly and let out a low whistle.

She smiled and told him he looked good, too. As they left and walked to his car, Cassie saw Jamie and Cindy outside in their driveway looking like they were in a heated discussion. Jamie looked over and did a double take at the two of them, or maybe it was just Cassie, and turned back to Cindy looking like he forgot what he was saying. Cindy looked over and let out a loud huff of annoyance and crossed her arms, practically tapping her foot, watching Cassie and Keith get in the car. What a freak.

"What's their deal?" Keith asked as he opened the door for Cassie.

"Who knows, who cares," she replied.

Although she did wonder about the two of them. They were engaged now yet every time she saw them outside or even a few run-ins at the supermarket, Jamie looked battered or annoyed. She knew he wasn't happy but wasn't sure he had the guts to leave Cindy. Their whole situation was too much to deal with let alone adding another address to his life. For now, Cassie just wanted to enjoy the night with Keith.

And she did just that. Their dinner was delicious. The restaurant was Cassie's favorite place for the food and the ambiance. They had never been there during the week but the energy inside made it feel like it was the weekend. There was a bar section with fairly loud and upbeat music but the dining room was in a separate area with jazz music playing at a moderate level. The lighting was romantic with softly lit chandeliers all around. She just loved it there.

Her mood was a little off though. She found herself not listening to Keith's stories like she usually did. He noticed after a few times but was too much of a gentleman to bring it up. Realizing she was being rude to him she snapped herself back and gave him her full attention.

The next surprise Keith had arranged was a horse drawn carriage to ride them around the downtown area. It was a perfect night for it with just the right amount of chill in the air to snuggle on the ride yet not too cold. The driver of the carriage had a blanket for them to share and Keith arranged it to lay across both their legs. There was also a hot chocolate dispenser if they wanted. The whole thing was like Santa's Sleigh. If it were the Christmas season the carriage would definitely be the thing to do. She decided she had to take Bailey on a ride during the holiday season once he got older. But for now, it was a really nice surprise.

They rode in silence with the sound of the horse's feet clopping down the road casting a white noise of sorts. The whole thing was relaxing. She leaned into Keith and looked up at the buildings. He squeezed her tight and kissed the top of her head.

Since they were downtown they rode past Brian's office building. She wondered if he were inside working or maybe out with Jane somewhere. This thought caught her off guard as she never wondered where Brian was before but figured that since she saw his building she would naturally wonder if he were there…..right? Fortunately there were many sights to see on the carriage ride so her and Keith started to make small talk and continue to enjoy the rest of the tour.

Overall the evening went by fairly uneventful which was fine with Cassie. Since it was a *surprise* evening she had been waiting for some announcement or maybe even proposal from Keith all night but nothing happened. She was glad for this and the silence on the ride home. For the past few days, ever since Brian came by with bagels, Cassie had felt a little off and wasn't sure why. She did have in the back of her mind that Brian was leaving and she was going to miss him for sure. And she also kept replaying the conversation she overheard with him and Bailey on the baby monitor. He was going to miss her, a lot. What did that mean? Should she talk to him about it or just let it go?

"Cassie," she heard Keith say a little annoyed.

"What?"

"I've been calling your name but you aren't answering. What are you thinking about?"

"Oh, sorry," she replied.

"What were you thinking about?" Keith asked again but this time with a little bit of annoyance in his voice. Oh boy. Maybe he's noticed her feeling off lately. Yikes.

"Oh, I was just thinking what a nice night this has been. Thank you, Keith. It was such a surprise. And very romantic!" She leaned over the seat and kissed his cheek.

He tilted his head towards the kiss but didn't say anything for a while. Cassie was starting to worry he did know something was on her mind, mainly Brian, but she also didn't have the energy to bring it up either and wasn't sure she really needed to. They drove on, neither were talking, and when they got to her house he walked her to the door. She thought he was going to spend the night as he often did so was surprised that he was already giving her a good night kiss on the front porch.

"Thanks for a great night, too, Cass. I'm glad you had a good time." He hugged her and started to pull away to leave.

"I did. But why aren't you staying over?"

Keith exhaled and looked away for a bit. When he looked back his eyes locked with hers and he didn't say anything for a while. She was too nervous to speak first so waited it out.

"I want to ask you a question and I want you to be very honest with me," Keith said. His hands held her by the arms as an emphasis of the importance of the question he was about to ask.

"Okay," replied Cassie slowly. Crap. He knows something is going on. But no way does he think it has anything to do with Brian. Cassie doesn't even know if her funky moods lately have anything to do with Brian.

"Is there something going on with you and Brian?" Keith asked slowly and without taking his eyes off hers.

What the --, thought Cassie. Unfortunately, she looked away and hesitated. When she looked back to answer him he was already pulling away.

"I knew something was going on. What exactly IS going on?" He was mad. Shit. She didn't know how things turned for the worse but she needed to back pedal fast.

"Nothing! Literally nothing is going on with Brian and me. Why are you asking me this?" She turned the tables around on Keith with her own question. She was starting to get pissed which wasn't helping in her back pedaling efforts. And she also noticed a light go on inside of Cindy's house. Great, an audience.

Before Keith could answer Cassie held a finger to her lips to silence him. She whispered that she saw a light go on and they needed to talk quieter. Keith didn't really say anything and watched Cassie go in the house but didn't follow her inside.

"I need to get going, I have an early meeting." He stepped inside and kissed her softly on the lips, touched his forehead to hers for a few moments, and then left. She watched him walk away, wanting him to turn back, yet she didn't call out to him.

Chapter 14

Over the next few days Cassie didn't see Keith at work. He had sent a text saying he was heading out of town to a clients and would call her when he came back. While she appreciate knowing he wasn't in the office, and selfishly didn't have to worry about running into him just yet, she also knew it wasn't how he usually acted. He would have told her he were leaving in person or at least would have called. Not just send a text. He was definitely annoyed. His question about her and Brian did surprise her though. Since she didn't know what to do she simply replied to him to have a nice trip and that was about all she could think of to say.

As planned, Brian called to make final arrangements for dinner before he left for London. She was looking forward to seeing Brian more than she wanted to and was glad Keith was out of town. She felt terrible thinking that way, too, but just didn't want to worry about Keith acting weird or jealous. Since they weren't really talking right now she didn't need to remind him about her dinner with Brian. At least that was how she justified it even though part of her didn't feel like she had to either.

Once again her parents had Bailey so she was able to take her time getting ready. She wasn't sure what to wear but knew they were going to a nice place downtown. For some reason she wanted to look really nice so opted for a little sapphire blue dress that she had been saving for a special occasion. The tags were still on it from over a year ago. She bought it while she was pregnant, wondering if she'd ever fit into it, and was happy to find out that it fit her nicely.

As for her hair, she usually wore it down but tonight she was going for a sultry look (yep, *sultry*, a more formal way of saying *sexy* by her definition) and wore it up with some wisps of hair escaping in all the right places. She did her make up as usual but added a slight shade darker lipstick and some extra eye liner. The final look in the mirror wasn't half bad.

When Brian arrived he looked not only handsome but happy. The last few times she saw him, aside from the morning he brought over bagels, he seem very distracted so it was nice to see him smile and look at ease. *He has a nice smile*, she thought. He looked her up and down and back up again and once he reached her eyes he literally paused and didn't say anything for a few moments.

"Wow, you look good," he said. Cassie almost blushed. She could tell he really meant it and was glad to know her extra effort in getting ready provided good results.

"Well, thank you. You look good, too," she said a little too flirtatious. His cologne wafted in the air and she wondered if he always wore cologne or if he put some on just for her. She decided to think it was just for her. Why not?

"Thanks. Well," he cleared his through, "okay then, let's go." He helped put her coat on and they walked out to the car. And just like the other evening when she was with Keith, she saw Jamie and Cindy outside in an obvious argument. They both stopped when they saw Brian and Cassie and this time Jamie actually yelled over and asked where they were going.

"To dinner," replied Brian flatly. Brian and Cassie got in the car and drove off with Jamie and Cindy staring after them silently.

Chapter 15

"What is their problem?" Brian asked the same question Keith did only a few nights ago.

"I really don't know. Anytime I see them they don't look happy. I feel bad for Lilly. I hope they're okay for her sake." She didn't like to see Jamie and Cindy at the start of what she had hoped would be a lovely night. They've ruined enough for her, they didn't need to ruin her last night with Brian before he left for who knows how long.

"Yeah, I know what you mean," Brian said in agreement. "I haven't seen Jamie happy in ages. I've asked him about it but he just blows me off and says everything's fine. Neither one of them seem happy. I'll bet Cindy is because she took Jamie from you but now that she has him who knows what she's thinking. I have to admit though they are one of the reasons I didn't want to go to London. I feel like I have to be here to protect Lilly from her crazy parents!" Brian let out a sad laugh and then sighed. "Well, let's talk about something else. I'm really happy we're doing this."

"Me, too. How have you been? Are you packed? Did you rent out your place?"

"I'm good. I'm actually getting excited for this move. Like I mentioned on the phone the other night the company provided movers and they basically did everything so that helped a lot. I ended up not packing my underwear and let them handle it all," Brian laughed and Cassie joined in. *Brian is such a guy*, she thought. She would never want a stranger going through her underwear drawer and packing her things up.

"And my company also found someone to rent my apartment out for a full year so I can decide closer to that time frame if I'm coming back or not," Brian said. "We'll see. One thing at a time I guess." He glanced over at her and her stomach did a little flip. Great.

"Yeah, I agree. It's the only way to handle such a big transition. I'm sure you'll love it over there and do a wonderful job, too. But Bailey and I will definitely miss Uncle Brian coming over." Cassie was surprised she said they would miss him but it's the truth, they would. She definitely would.

They were at a light and he looked over at her and said, "I'm going to miss you guys, too." And kept staring at her until the person behind them tapped their horn.

Cassie felt herself blush again, a lot! Ok, what she heard on the monitor the other day was what she had secretly hoped it was. She was torn between excitement and surprise at why this confirmation made her happy. What did it mean? What about Keith? But what about Brian going to London? It didn't make a difference though. He was going across the pond and she wouldn't see him for maybe a whole year. Did she want him to stay? Was it even her choice? Of course it wasn't.

They had nothing going on between them except a strong friendship and apparent attraction. All he said was he was going to miss her and Bailey and she started to mentally freak. She knew he would miss them. He'd also miss his niece, Lilly, and Jamie, too. The list goes on for a long time of who he will miss. Her emotions were suddenly getting the better of her and she looked out the window and tried to compose herself before he noticed anything. Her phone pinged that she had a text so she fished around for it in her purse. The text was from Jamie. *What the hell?*

"I just got a text from Jamie," she told Brian.

"Really? What's it say?" He asked.

"He wrote that he wants to talk to me. He said for me to text him when I get home later. This is strange," she said slowly.

"Uh, yeah it is," agreed Brian. "Are you going to reply?"

"Yeah, I'm asking what he wants." She sent the message back and held her phone waiting for his reply. Jamie knew she was going out to dinner with Brian. He knew it was going to be later when she got home. Why is he trying to finagle a stupid text into her and Brian's night out? Was he jealous? She hoped not because the idea of Jamie thinking he had any right to be jealous pissed her off.

"That's strange. Why would he text you now? He knows we're out to dinner," Brian basically spoke out loud all that Cassie was thinking. "Do you think he's jealous?" Another question that had already popped into Cassie's head.

"I don't know why he would be. We haven't been together for close to two years. Plus he'd been with Cindy for who knows how long before I found out. Maybe he wants to talk about Bailey or even Lilly." She was giving Jamie the benefit of the doubt but also knew he wasn't happy with Cindy. Regardless, his text came at a really annoying time and she believed he knew it, too.

The phone pinged again and she read the text out loud. "It says, 'I just want to talk to you. I've wanted to for a while now but I've been too scared to come over.'" And before she could turn her shocked face to Brian the phone pinged with one more text that said, "I want you back.'"

Neither Brian nor Cassie spoke. They just looked at each other for a moment. Brian turned to keep his eyes on the road. Cassie was stunned. Is this for real? A part of her thought Cindy had Jamie's phone and was testing to see what she would say. But another part of her had a feeling that Jamie did miss her, at least that he was unhappy with Cindy.

Brian drove the car into a parking garage and turned into a spot and shut off the engine. He shifted in his seat and turned to look at her slouching backward against the side door looking shocked. "What the hell, Cass. Do you think that's from him or maybe Cindy playing one of her games?"

"I don't know, I thought the same thing." She was still holding the phone in her hand, not sure what to do. If this was from Jamie, was she happy or pissed? She didn't think she was happy but when your ex wants you back there is a little thrill involved. Did she feel numb? She didn't know.

Her phone pinged again and Brian sat up and waited for her to read the text. She looked at her phone and said, "Um, this one is from Keith." Brian had no idea that she and Keith were going through something and she didn't want to bring it up either. She read it silently to herself and then sat back in her seat. She started to chuckle and said, "Keith said he wants to talk to me and asked if I'm home."

Once again neither of them said anything. They sat in silence for a full minute before Brian finally spoke. "Cass, if you want to go home and deal with all of this I understand. We can try to go out again before I leave for London for a lunch or something. I don't want you to feel pressured for us to go out tonight."

Cassie didn't know what to say. She was touched at Brian's sensitivity to whatever was happening. She didn't want to go home. She knew that much.

"No," Cassie said easily. "I want to be here, with you..."

Brian let out a little gasp as if he'd been holding his breath. It was adorable! She smiled slightly. He did, too. As if they both knew what was coming, they leaned toward each other and kissed. Softly at first but then more urgent. She couldn't believe how natural it felt, how nice it felt, how good he smelled and tasted which was like minty toothpaste. He pulled away and looked at her, tossed her phone to the floor of the car and then held her in his arms as if protecting her from the cell phone and the annoying texts.

"Cassie," was all he said. It was enough. She knew of all three men in her life right now, Brian, Keith and Jamie, Brian was the one she wanted to be with at that moment. But he was leaving for a long time at least. And Keith and she were in a relationship. And Jamie, whom she had shared her life with and has a child with, lived next door. What was happening at this instant with Brian was too much to add to her plate. To his plate. But it also made her feel content. Almost peaceful.

"Brian, I don't know what to do," was all she could say. She could feel him nodding and they just held each other. They finally pulled back and both had tears in their eyes.

"Cassie, I'm sorry. We both have a lot going on and I'm sorry to throw this in the mix. But I've had feelings for you for so long now. I couldn't tell you though cause of Jamie and obviously Keith. And Jane." He looked down and shook his head. "I'm sorry," he repeated.

"Don't be sorry. I'm not," she put her finger under his chin and lifted his face to look at her. "I've had feelings for you too but wasn't being honest with myself. But here we are and I'm not sorry. I don't know what that means but I'm not. All I know is that you're leaving for London soon. And that I'm hungry," she smiled and so did Brian. "Let's go eat and change the subject. For now. It's just too overwhelming."

"Okay, you're right. Let's go. Do you want to reply to them though?" He tilted his head toward the phone on the floor.

"I guess so at least to avoid more texts from them. I'd like to turn my phone off but can't in case my parents call about Bailey."

"Right, of course."

"I'm not sure what to say to either of them. Any suggestions?" She asked.

"No, not really, sorry." His face was so tender and caring. She wanted to kiss him again but didn't. They needed to step back and get their thoughts and emotions in order. Get back to a good frame of mind.

"I know. I'm just going to reply to Jamie that we can talk another time and I'm also going to say that he is crazy," she said with exaggeration. "And I'm going to tell Keith that I'm out and we can talk over the weekend." As she was saying this she was also texting them back. She avoided mentioning Brian's name to Keith. She felt bad about this but needed to stop the madness. She wondered if Brian noticed. Anyway, this evening was about Brian and, regardless of their kiss, she didn't want Jamie or Keith to ruin the night for them. Cassie was usually very sensitive to other people's feelings but this time she was a little bit mad at Keith for the way he left things the last time they saw each other. She was starting to feel overwhelmed again and needed to get out of the car. Smelling Brian's cologne in the air snapped her back to the present and she put her phone back in her purse and said," Let's go."

Chapter 16

Dinner with Brian was wonderful. The restaurant had a romantic yet fun vibe. It was a large room separated into a bar area in the front and a dining area towards the back with the kitchen hidden off to the side. The ceilings were high and pretty chandeliers gave off just enough lighting to keep the place dimly lit. Candles on the tables were emphasized because of the slight darkness to the room. And soft jazzy music played from the overhead speaker system.

Cassie kept her phone on the table to the side incase her parents needed her about Bailey. At first both she and Brian were aware the phone was there and could go off at any minute, but after their first drink they started to relax and the conversation went from how nice the restaurant was to various topics including the move to London. Brian was on a good career track at his company and the transfer to London showed faith on both his and his boss's side.

While he was talking her mind went to their kiss and then to his leaving. For a year! She had to stop from thinking too far ahead. Brian looked at her often without saying anything and she knew he was probably thinking the same things as she was.

The dinner lasted for almost two hours and their time together was full of laughter and smiles. She hadn't laughed that much in a long time. Jamie and her laughed and had a good time when they were dating in college but who didn't in that phase of life? Everyone laughs in college.

After they graduated and married things were still good but then both their careers started to get serious and he eventually started to sleep with their neighbor so, you know, the fun sort of died out. Keith made her laugh often but there was something about Brian. It wasn't that Brian was a jokester, he really wasn't, but he told good stories and had a dry sense of humor. Plus he was easy on the eyes. Big time. Keith and Jamie were both handsome but more in that pretty boy way. Brian had the looks and a physicality that was, for lack of any other word, delicious. Anyone looking at him for the first time would know he had been athletic back in the day and still kept fitness as part of his daily routine. He still participated in a variety of Cross Fit competitions, too. Yep, easy on the eyes.

Brian paid the check and instead of walking back to the car they went for a stroll around the wide river that wound through the surrounding area. The downtown region was stunning. Even though she had been down there recently with Keith they hadn't walked along the water. The lights of the buildings reflected off the river and well lit walkways with weather worn gas lamps were all around. They weren't the only ones out enjoying the night. Couples and even families were all over. Cassie was surprised at the amount of people this late on a weeknight but she was usually in her pajamas by 9 pm and in bed by 10 pm so what did she know?

Brian grabbed her hand to stop her from walking and pulled her close to kiss her again. This time was even nicer since they weren't in the car. She let it happen, allowing her mind, guilt and confusion to slip away. He eventually put his arm around her and they looked out at the skyline across the river. It really was spectacular. They didn't speak for a while but finally one of them had to so Brian did the honors.

"I had a great night, Cass. I didn't expect things to go the way they did but I'm glad. I'm really going to miss you when I leave. I miss you already." He hugged her again. She liked his hugs.

"I know and I'm going to miss you, too." They kept silent for a while longer until Cassie asked the inevitable question, "What are we going to do?"

"I don't know… I really don't know," he said sadly. "All I know is I need to go to *London*. And it sounds like you need to deal with Jamie *and* Keith. And I'm also going to have to think about Jane. I don't want to hurt her or my brother. Or Keith. He's a great guy," his voice trailed off. "I have a big job waiting for me across the pond and I'll be so busy. To be honest, I really don't know what to do or say right now. I hope you understand," he said affectionately.

"Yes, I understand and I agree. This thing between us, whatever it is, is new and it isn't fair to anyone if we don't address the other relationships involved. I'm in a relationship with a great guy and you're in one with a great girl. And then we have Jamie, my ex and your brother. I don't know what's going to happen with us, or us and anyone else, but I think maybe London is a good way to step back and see how we really feel. I know I feel strongly for you but to be honest it surprises me, I need to know if it's real and not just because I can't have you. We have a friendship that means so much to me and I don't want to lose that either. Does all of this make sense?" She hoped she wasn't rambling on making zero sense but needed to think out loud.

"Yeah, it makes perfect sense. I've had feelings for you for a long time but the timing was never right. Or at least I didn't think it was. I guess I never wanted to cross that line. And Keith and Jane are great people. Jamie is a pain in the ass," he chuckled, "but still my brother. I don't want to hurt anyone either. All I know is I *do not* know what is going to happen and that I will definitely miss you and just spending time with you."

"Me, too," replied Cassie sadly. They stood there looking out at the sights for a while longer. Finally, Brian kissed her on the forehead and led the way back to the car. They drove back in silence and he pulled in her driveway all too soon. Each knew their fairytale night was over and that the next time they saw each other, when he came by to see Bailey and Lilly before he left for London, others would be around and there wouldn't be a chance to be alone. He walked her to the door, gave her another hug, no kiss this time, and left. From inside her front window she watched him drive away as a tear fell silently down her cheek.

Chapter 17

Early the next morning Cassie's parents came by with Bailey and had brought breakfast, too. They couldn't stay long and she still had to get herself ready for work for an impromptu meeting her boss put on the schedule. Pepper was coming over to watch Bailey and planned to take him and Lilly to the zoo. Cassie was excited for the kids to have a fun day. But she didn't feel like going to work.

Cassie felt like she wasn't running on full steam, still feeling heavy about the night before. Any help she could get to keep Bailey entertained she appreciated. She was nervous to see Keith although wasn't even sure if he would be there. At the same time she was also eager to address things head on. Another bagel, cup of coffee and sloppy kiss from Bailey and she was ready for the day.

Once she got to the office she dialed Joe's extension. She hadn't seen him in a long time and missed his flamboyant energy. He definitely did not disappoint as he came into her office with a brightly flowered shirt on, cuffs up to reveal a pattern not at all like the shirt, and a deep orange pair of pants. His shoes were black.

"CASS!!!!!!!!!!!" Joe roared. Cassie laughed and got up from her chair to hug him. His bear hug enveloped her in his signature cologne he had been wearing for years. She closed her eyes and welcomed the hominess of his scent.

"Hi Joe, I've missed you! How are you? How's Jack?"

"Jack is great! Guess what….we're moving in together! I've been trying to catch you at the office to tell you but it's been a crazy past few weeks. And I don't want to bother you at home at night when you're with Bailey. And how is Mr. Bailey?" She was touched that he asked about Bailey knowing full well that all he wanted to do was talk about Jack.

"Oh, Joe, I'm so happy for you! I'm so glad you two are taking things to the next level. And Bailey is great, already has two teeth coming in, getting too big too fast."

"I want to come by soon and see him. Hey, what are you doing this weekend?"

"Well, I should be home but Brian is coming by to say good bye to Bailey and Lilly. He's moving to London for a year, at least. Did I tell you that?"

"Uh, nooooooooo! You didn't mention to me that handsome, yummy Brian is leaving the country! He was half the reason I would come visit you when you were pregnant since he was over your house so often! I always, always, always hoped you two would get together so I could live vicariously through you! He is so delicious…," Joe said and literally twirled around the room as if in a dream.

Cassie laughed. "Whoa, Joe, I had no idea you thought Brian was *that* hot *OR* that you wanted he and I to get together. Since when?" She was really surprised and wondered how long he had been thinking this way.

"Duh, Cass," Joe said. He stuck his head out of the office door, turned it this way and that, checking the hallway, and came back and said quietly, "Keith is great, but he isn't for you. Brian is." He finished his proclamation with a quick nod of his head as if to say his word is final, no questions asked.

"Are you serious?" Asked a truly stunned Cassie.

Joe looked at Cassie for a moment before answering. "Yes." Another nod.

"Joe, I have something to tell you." She got up and shut her office door, also checking the hallway before doing so, and sat back down.

"Brian and I kissed last night. We went to dinner. Had a great time. And kissed. A couple of times." It felt good to finally tell someone.

Joe once again just stared at Cassie. He didn't seem to be blinking. Then he leaned forward and said urgently, "How was it?"

"It was nice," she said with the same emotion she would use to comment on the weather. Joe almost threw a stapler at her.

Adamantly, yet quietly, Joe somewhat roared, "Nice!? You kissed HOT Brian and it was 'nice'?! I want details, woman!"

Cassie laughed once again and told Joe more details. She loved how she could tell him anything. Unfortunately that went both ways and let's just say Cassie knew way too much information about gay men and what they did behind closed doors.

Their conversation was interrupted by a knock on the door. It was one of their co-workers reminding them both of the meeting about to start in less than five minutes with the Divisional Head of the Department. No way should anyone be late.

"Oh wow! I almost forgot! Thanks, Mimi!" Cassie said while looking down at her desk.

She gathered her papers, shut down her computer, grabbed her cell and she and Joe rushed down the hallway to the conference room. As she turned the corner she ran right into Keith's chest. Papers flew all over and she, Keith and Joe helped picked them up.

Her cell phone had fallen, too, and as they were picking up the papers it pinged with the screen showing a message from Brian. Gulp. Keith saw it and gave Cassie a look. She looked away and gathered more papers and her phone and went into the conference room. Everyone seemed a little late so were still taking seats. She sat down and Joe was on one side of her and Keith on the other.

"Aren't you going to read your text from Brian?" Keith leaned over and whispered to her a little annoyingly.

"Oh, uh, yeah," she replied sounding like a guilty idiot. The text simply said he'd stop by tomorrow with Jane to see Bailey and Lilly and asked if that was okay for them.

She then triumphantly read the text to Keith as if to say she wasn't worried that the text was from Brian professing his love for her but just a friendly reminder of his coming to see his niece and nephew… With his girlfriend… Whatever.

Keith didn't have a chance to reply as the Divisional Manager walked in and began the meeting. Cassie barely heard anything he said because all she could think about was why Brian was bringing Jane. But what did she expect?

They had both said they needed to sort things out, whether with each other or their current partner. Jane was good with Bailey and Lilly so she probably wanted to see them too before Brian took off. It's not like she'd come by on her own and visit with them once he was in London.

Cassie needed to settle down and stop acting like a smitten school girl. So she changed her thoughts and started to think about what she should wear when Brian came over. Yeah, she was off to a good start.

Chapter 18

Since Brian was leaving on a late flight the day after next Cassie decided to make sort of an impromptu surprise going away party for him. The plan was that Brian and Jane were coming over to see Bailey at Cassie's house and then head over to see Lilly next door. Cassie bit the bullet and invited Jamie, Cindy and Lilly over as well Joe, Jack and Keith. She decided to act like all was fine with all of them as opposed to an upcoming episode of The Jerry Springer Show. And she chose to act as if she and Keith were going strong and she hadn't just cheated on him by making out with Brian. Or that Jamie hadn't sent a text saying he missed her. As if Cindy wasn't a pain in the ass. And as if she and Brian never shared a kiss, or two.

She had replied to Brian's text after her meeting and wrote for him and Jane to come by around 5 and to be hungry. After work she ran to the grocery store and bought food and drink, small votive candles for the table setting and a few balloons. Why not? This was a bon voyage party and a party needed balloons and music. She hoped it would be a nice gathering of people minding their manners. Regardless of her and Brian's latest romp she knew he was sad to leave and hoped everyone would be on their best behavior and that he'd have a good time.

When she finally went home Pepper stayed a bit longer and they shared a glass of wine and chatted for a bit. She told Pepper about the "surprise" party for Brian the next day and hoped they could be there, too. Pepper said they definitely would. This was good, Cassie thought. The more the merrier. She would have invited her parents, too, but they had taken off for an out of town mini vacation that morning.

Pepper left and just as Cassie was about to take Bailey up for his bath there was a knock at the door. She and Bailey opened it to find Keith standing there. Quickly Bailey reached for him and Keith took him easily. She was surprised Bailey missed Keith but then again they did have a good relationship. It was really quite sweet.

"Hey, Bay, how ya doing?" Keith said to Bailey.

Bailey smiled and cooed his reply. He was starting to say a few "words" like "Mah" for Mom or "FiFi" for Sophie. Bailey seemed to do a hard K sound when he saw Keith so she figured he would say his name in no time. It was so sweet to watch him grow.

Cassie shut the door and offered Keith a drink. He declined and asked what they were doing. She told him that they were about to head up for Bailey's bath and

Keith said he would help. Cassie didn't really need the help but didn't want to hurt his feelings. They went up and gave Bailey his bath and got him ready for bed. They took turns reading books to him like a happy couple while he drank his bottle and feel asleep in Cassie's arms. Once he was in a deep sleep she laid him in his crib and Keith left them alone, knowing Cassie liked to look at him while he slept.

When she came downstairs, Keith was at the kitchen table with two glasses of wine in front of him. She took hers and sat down opposite him. She always had music playing softly on her IPod on the kitchen counter so the silence wasn't so bad. And she wasn't about to speak first.

"So," began Keith, "I'm glad we have this time alone to talk. How are you?"

"I'm good. I'm sorry I wasn't available last night when you texted me," She said with a trace of guilt. "Brian and I went to dinner like we planned. Remember I told you we were going to do that?" She was glad it was out and felt herself holding her breath waiting to see what he'd say.

"Oh, right, I wasn't sure when that would be," he said a little sad. *Ugh*, she thought. She didn't want to hurt his feelings. She knew enough that she really did care for Keith and didn't want him sad or even mad but still wasn't sure if her feelings were due to love or friendship or even guilt.

"Yeah, we had a nice time," she said breezily to erase any thoughts of romance from Keith's mind. So she basically lied to him. "I was going to text you but wasn't sure how you'd react considering how we left things the other night..." Her voice trailed off and she sort of looked away. So did Keith.

"I'm sorry about that, Cass. I just had to ask. I felt like something was going on with you and Brian. Before you and I started our relationship I recall your saying many times how Brian was there for you during your breakup with Jamie and while you were pregnant with Bailey. I know he means a lot to you. He's a really great guy so it doesn't surprise me. I know you two are close so I thought maybe something was brewing up..."

"Brewing up?" Cassie laughed a little and without looking Keith in the eye said, "No, nothing is 'brewing up' but I understand where the question comes from." She felt guilty for not admitting that maybe something WAS brewing up or starting to happen but she still wasn't sure what was going on with her and Brian so left it at that.

"Okay, well, thanks for letting me talk about it with you. I'm glad nothing is going on," he said with a little smile. She looked at him and gave a half assed smile back, unsure of what to do next.

Keith took care of that and walk over to her, took her by the hand, and started to slow dance with her right there in the kitchen to the music playing in the background. It was a simple yet romantic gesture. She was still bothered but actually felt something stir inside of her, something she hadn't felt for Keith in a while. Interesting. Maybe she needed to give her and Keith's relationship more attention, more effort. She owed him that much. Yes, she had feelings for Brian but there were a lot of hurdles involved. One being the huge ass ocean that would be in between them in a few days. And Jamie was the other hurdle.

But regardless, it wasn't fair to toss her relationship with Keith aside and run to Brian. Maybe it was just a crush she had for Brian and him for her. They had been friends for years and while she thought he was a unique man in many ways was that enough to hurt so many people involved? Keith was here, he was dreamy, great with Bailey and overall a wonderful person. She was lucky to be in a relationship with him and suddenly felt ashamed at what she did with Brian. Granted, she was no fool and not about to tell Keith this, but she definitely felt bad. She and Keith continued to dance some more and had a romantic rest of the night. She fell asleep easily in his arms and dreamt of swimming across the Atlantic Ocean. Crap.

Chapter 19

The next morning Bailey woke Cassie and Keith up bright and early. She was glad Keith was there for a number of reasons. The first reason being he was able to help with Bailey in the morning while she sat down with a cup of coffee and her TO DO list to get things in order for the party. She could easily handle Bailey on her own but since she was hosting a party in a few hours she needed all the help she could get. She told Keith about the party the night before and he thought it was a great idea and didn't even sound jealous, thank God!

Keith was a marvel in the kitchen so had a few good suggestions of what to make. He helped straighten up the house, kept Bailey occupied, decorated, washed glasses, chose the music and helped her with some of the food dishes she was making. He ran back to his place to get clean clothes even though he had a lot of his things at her house. She noticed an extra kick in his step, probably from their moving past this Brian saga.

When Keith came back he had a wrapped present. She thought it was for her but he said it was for Brian from the two of them. Being the thoughtful guy he was, as it turned out, when he ran back to his place he stopped off at a specialty store and bought Brian a going away gift. He played it off as if the gift was not a big deal but Keith often spared no expense. Sure enough, it was a simple leather bound notepad with refills and Brian's initials engraved in the bottom corner. It was a great gift for someone in Brian's position. With all the responsibilities that Brian was about to undergo in London, having a nice TO DO list pad was going to come in handy.

Time had flown by and Cassie still needed to hop in the shower and get ready. Fortunately Keith kept Bailey occupied so she was able to spend a little more time on her appearance. She came back down dressed in a casual pair of dark blue skinny jeans that fit her in all the right places and a black form fitting turtle neck sweater with dark brown leather boots. She wore her hair down and wavy and had on hoop earrings. Keith did a double take at her and did his characteristic low whistle sound, following by a soft and slow and passionate kiss on the lips. Whoa, thought Cassie. Her head actually started to spin a little from the kiss. She smiled happily knowing that Keith still had that effect on her. He looked nice in his designer jeans, a charcoal gray cashmere sweater and casual leather shoes. Plus she smelled a hint of his cologne. He definitely looked good.

Keith had Bailey all dressed for the party in his little khaki pants and navy blue long sleeved dress shirt. He looked adorable. They had set up the extra-large playpen in the family room in case Bailey and Lilly got fussy and needed a break from the grown-ups. As if on cue, the doorbell rang and guests started to arrive. She had everyone come a half hour before Brian and Jane and it worked out great. People also brought gifts which she hadn't asked them to do but was certainly happy that they did. The party was really going to mean a lot to Brian and that meant a great deal to her.

On time Brian and Jane arrived and she could tell Brian was truly surprised. Cassie had called Jane to give her the heads up on the party so she understandably knew what to expect and was helpful in getting him there on time. Brian could be late due to his work and she didn't want them missing a good window of time with the babies before they got cranky for the night. So far the party was a success. Only a few more hours to go.

And the party did continue on nicely. There were only two hiccups of the night. The first was that Jamie caught Cassie in the kitchen alone and asked her what she thought of his text the other night.

"Jamie, are you kidding me? This is a party. There are people ten feet away. I'm not going to have this conversation with you right now. Maybe not ever," she whispered with a hint of being pissed. She had been gathering more food to put out on the table and did not need him distracting her.

"Cass, I really miss you though. Come on, let's go outside and talk." He had a slur to his words and she realized he may have had too much to drink. He started to approach her and she backed into the kitchen counter, not sure which way to turn. At that moment Brian came in and saw what was happening. He swiftly and quietly backed Jamie away and took him outside for some fresh air. As he was walking Jamie out Brian looked back at Cassie with a sad smile. All she could do was return the same smile. At that moment Keith came in to see if she needed any help and saw the look on her face. She realized she hadn't told him about the text from Jamie so filled him in on what Jamie had written to her the other day. He listened and when she was finished he looked her in the eye and said he knew that this would eventually happen.

"What do you mean"? She asked.

He looked over his shoulder to make sure no one was around, turned back and whispered to her, "Cindy can be a real pain in the ass and he knows it now. And even if she wasn't, I can't imagine him not missing you at some point and wishing he could turn back time and be with you again."

"You really think so?" Her voice almost sounded hopeful but that wasn't what she was feeling. Yes, at one point Jamie missing her was all that she wanted, but hearing it now was almost sad.

"Yes, I do. You are an exceptional woman and any man, myself included, would love to have you in their life. Trust me, you're a catch," he smiled.

She blushed and told him the same thing back. They kissed each other and as they were about to pull away, Brian walked in the back door and stopped. The second hiccup of the night.

"Oh, sorry, I didn't mean to interrupt," and he quickly left the kitchen.

"See, Cass. Any man." Keith gave her a small smile, grabbed one of the serving trays and left, leaving her alone in the kitchen with a mind full of confusion and guilt.

Chapter 20

The next morning Bailey slept late which allowed Cassie to lay in bed and think of the night before. The party had been a success and everyone could tell Brian was appreciative of their being there and the gifts they brought. Joe and Jack had a good time and entertained everyone who would listen with stories of their circle of friends and explaining to Brian and Jamie's parents what a "drag queen" was and how it doesn't' necessarily mean a person is gay. Pepper and her husband were so curious they continued to ask questions as they walked out of the door at the end of the night.

Cindy had been on her semi-best behavior and even stayed after Brian told her he took Jamie home. She and Lilly were almost the last to leave. Cassie could tell Cindy needed to cut loose. She drank too much and had definitely hit on Brian, Keith and even Joe and Jack. Yes, Joe and Jack. She was out of control. Brian and Jane walked her and Lilly home and even put Lilly to bed as Cindy seemed a little too tipsy to navigate the front stoop let alone a baby on a changing table.

And the last to leave were Brian and Jane. Brian caught Cassie alone in the kitchen and gave her a hug and thanked her for the night. He had to be at the airport that evening. His flight was due to leave around midnight and it had been late by the time everyone left so he didn't have much time. Jane would take him to the airport. Cassie had tears in her eyes as they hugged and neither had much to say. They heard Keith and Jane heading towards the kitchen so broke apart, still looking sheepish to anyone who saw them.

"Well, thank you so much for the lovely evening, Cassie. And Keith. We had a great time," Jane said.

"Oh, of course, I'm glad you two had a good time," Cassie replied. She and Jane gave each other a quick and awkward hug and turned their attention to Brian and Keith.

"Well, we should get going then," Brian said and turned to shake Keith's hand. "Thanks again for the gift, man, I was really touched. It'll definitely come in handy over there."

"No problem, glad you like it." They did one of those half hugs/loud slaps on the backs that guys do. Very macho.

The four of them walked to the front door and Brian and Cassie hugged once more. Keith and Jane had been within a foot of each side of them so the hug lacked any emotion but that was probably for the better. She saw tears in Brian's eyes as he turned away. Cassie had them, too. Keith left her alone while she stood in the doorway to watch them drive away. She knew she would be sad when Brian left but didn't think it would hurt as bad as it did.

Chapter 21

The next few weeks went by as normal as any Cassie could remember. She hadn't heard from Brian except for a group text sent to herself, Pepper and Jamie, saying he had made it to London and that all was going well. She presumed Jane received a private, more personal text, since she wasn't on the group text. Whatever. She was undeniably bothered by this imagined romantic triangle but after a few days of being cranky, she accepted, once again, that it was for the best that she and Brian continue as "friends" and not dwell on their possible romantic feelings. And even if they did try to have a relationship there was always the chance it didn't work out and then their friendship would be over, tainted. She did not want that to happen. So the more she thought about it the more she wanted to work on her and Keith's relationship. At least she convinced herself that she did.

One day after work Cassie and Bailey had been upstairs playing in his room when she heard the doorbell. She and Bailey went downstairs and opened the door to find Jamie standing there. He looked like he just came from the office from the looks of his suit, loosened tie and briefcase in his hand.

"Hey," he said to Cassidy, sounding a little sad about something. He touched Bailey's check very tenderly but Bailey turned away and motioned to be let down.

"Hey, what's up?" Cassie put Bailey down and he toddled off to the family room to play with some toys he had in there. She wished Bailey had given Jamie even a little bit of attention but then again he was at an age where he wasn't in the habit of being considerate.

"Um, I need to talk to you about something," Jamie said. Cassie rolled her eyes at him. "Just a few minutes is all I'm asking for," he said quickly.

Cassie looked at Jamie oddly but stepped aside and let him in. He went to the kitchen, opened the fridge and grabbed himself a beer. *Okay, help yourself*, she thought. He sat down at the kitchen table and took a big swig of the bottle. He looked uncomfortable. She sat down, too, and waited it out.

Finally, after what seemed like a silly amount of silence, Jamie said, "I miss you."

Now it was Cassie's turn to be uncomfortable. "What?"

"I miss you. A lot. Things with Cindy aren't working out and even if they were, I miss you," he said and then took another drink of his beer. He must be drinking for courage. "Do you miss me?"

Uh.

"Do you?" he asked again.

"No, not really…" She actually felt bad saying it but wanted to be honest. He looked surprised and hurt at the same time. But, she needed to say what she was about to say.

"Jamie, let me explain," she tried to make him look at her but he was sitting back in his chair with his hand in his hair looking at the ceiling. "Listen," she continued, "I did miss you at first and it hurt for a long time. You hurt me bad, Jamie," she said and tried to make him look at her. She needed him to hear what she wanted to say. He finally looked at her with angry eyes.

"But, surprisingly," she continued, "the pain didn't last as long as I thought it would. You and I were already growing apart by the time I found out about you and Cindy so when it happened, when you guys told me what was going on, I don't know, it hurt, yeah, and I was crushed. But I couldn't stay in that mindset for long. I had to take care of myself because I was pregnant with Bailey. And then time just went by." She found herself looking across the room at Bailey playing with his shaping toys. The peace she felt looking at him erased how gloomy the conversation was with Jamie.

She turned back and continued. "I'm sorry, Jamie. I definitely had a lot of sad moments, I did. And I cried a lot but, honestly, I didn't as much as I thought I would. I think we were over before we were officially over. I'm just being honest with you, Jamie. I really am sorry." Cassie found it ironic that she was apologizing to Jamie over what happened but did feel empathetic towards him.

"You didn't love me?" Jamie seemed to be getting almost mad so Cassie had to back pedal to keep him calmed down.

"Of course I loved you! That's a stupid question, Jamie. Of course I did. But you know that we grew apart. I guess you were too busy to notice because you were sneaking around with Cindy but we were not as close as we had been back in college and when we first got married," she said with a surprising lack of scorn.

Jamie didn't say anything for a while. He just sipped his beer and looked off in the distance. While Cassie was surprised and uncomfortable with their conversation and his being there, at the table, a few feet from her, she knew they had to have this talk. And she said pretty much all that she wanted to say. So once again she waited it out until Jamie finally spoke.

He turned towards her and said, "Well, I miss you. Do you think we could try to work things out?" He said this as if none of what Cassie had said made any difference. As if they could just ignore her feelings, or lack of, and plow forward.

Cassie almost laughed but didn't. Jamie appeared serious and solemn. "Um, no Jamie, I'm sorry. We are way past that point. I definitely want to have a good relationship with you so we can raise Bailey together but that is all. And let's not forget that I'm in a serious relationship with Keith and you're in one with Cindy." *And I made out with your brother*, she thought to herself.

"Well, I'm not going to give up on us, Cass. I made a mistake and I'm sorry, too. And I'm sorry that it took me this long to apologize to you for all that I did to us, to our family. I really am," he looked off into the distance again. "Cindy is a pain in the ass sometimes. But she's my daughter's mother. And you're my son's mother. It's so messed up. I really messed things up," Jamie said sadly while slowly shaking his head.

"Yeah, you did, Jamie. I really don't know what to tell you," Cassie said as kindly as she could.

Jamie slowly got up, put the beer bottle on the kitchen counter, and walked to the door. Cassie followed him to the foyer and Jamie suddenly turned around, grabbed Cassie by her arms, and kissed her. She tried to pull away but he held her tighter, stepping forward with his hips, kissing her as if his life depended on it. She didn't kiss him back but stopped trying to pull away from him, hoping he would loosen his grip. It worked and she pulled away, stepped back and instinctively put her hand to her mouth.

"Jamie, what the hell was that?" Cassie was pissed. She felt violated. She had told him she didn't want to patch things up with him, she was with Keith and he was with Cindy. There was no need for that.

Jamie grinned at her and rubbed his hand down his tie to smooth it out. He straightened his suit jacket, grabbed his briefcase, and looked at her again. "That was nice," he said simply.

"Jamie! Are you nuts? Don't ever do that again," Cassie said as loud as she could without Bailey overhearing her or the neighbors either. Had he heard *anything* that she said to him?

"We'll see," he said too damn confidently. He turned and left her standing there dumbfounded.

What the hell.

Chapter 22

Cassie didn't hear from Jamie for days after he kissed her. And she was glad about that. It annoyed her that he had seemed too smug, too confident, like he was playing her or had some plan to woo her to him. She didn't like it one bit. A few times after the *incident*, as she liked to refer to it as, she saw him, Cindy and their baby outside but just waved and kept going. *How odd*, she thought. Without a doubt there was going to be quite a fireworks show when or if Cindy ever found out about Jamie wanting Cassie back. She definitely didn't want to be a fly on that wall. It was bad enough she was right next door.

Keith and Cassie spent a lot of time together in general but it seemed to be increasing. Ever since Brian left for London Keith seemed more confident in his and Cassie's relationship and came around more often. It was nice for Bailey to have a male figure around besides Jamie so Cassie was glad. Cindy demanded so much of his time that it was hard for Jamie to see his son as much as he wanted. This annoyed Cassie to no end but there wasn't much she could do about it except be there for Bailey as both the mommy AND the daddy. She missed Brian coming around. Brian was Bailey's uncle and Keith was, who? His mommy's special friend? She wasn't sure how to label Keith and Bailey's relationship but was at least glad that Keith was a positive influence in her son's life.

Brian hadn't reached out to Cassie at all except for that first group text saying he arrived safely. She sent him a reply individually saying she was glad he was there safe and to keep in touch but he hadn't replied yet. A part of her was glad because she just didn't know what their communicating would do, what their end game would be and what it would do to their friendship that meant so much to her. On the other hand, she did want to hear from him. Their kiss was weeks and weeks ago and it meant a lot to her but maybe it didn't mean as much to him after all. She wasn't sure what to think and was actually getting tired of thinking about it if she were honest with herself. Regardless, she didn't want to bother him because she knew he had a lot to do to get his new office up and running in the UK.

Cassie threw herself into Bailey, her work and her time with Keith. She also went out to dinner with Joe a few times which she always enjoyed. He was so happy which made her happy, too. Things were really working out for Joe and Jack and they were talking about marriage. During one of their outings Cassie told Joe about Jamie kissing her. He gasped and was just as shocked as she had been and asked his million and one questions. Once the surprise wore off he told her to watch out since Jamie seemed a little delusional and that Cindy was border line off balance.

The recipe of Jamie's feelings for Cassie, Cindy's feelings for Jamie and Cassie's feelings for Keith, and maybe Brian, were not a good mix. Cassie knew Joe was right and while she hadn't done anything since Jamie's kiss she did want to let Keith know. That was not a conversation she was looking forward to considering how jealous he got over Brian but she had to tell him before it came up in another way.

One warm summer night Keith came over and cooked out on the grill. Bailey had been adorable as always and tired out easily since he had eaten practically a whole hamburger and lots of fruit and had played most of the afternoon. After she put him to bed she decided to let Keith know about Jamie. She came back outside with the baby monitor in hand and Keith handed her a beer for her other hand. She thanked him and sat down by the pit fire he had started. It had probably been too warm for a fire but both enjoyed the solace that it brought.

"Hey, Keith, I need to talk to you about something," Cassie said. She had taken a sip of her beer and stared at the fire for a while. She sensed that he wasn't going to rush her so they both watched the fire, mesmerized by its flickering flames and occasional crackle. The silence was comfortable.

After a long time Cassie finally sat straighter in her chair and told Keith what happened with Jamie. She was quick to add her lack of feelings for him and that the few times she had seen him since then he hadn't acknowledged the kiss but did wink at her once when he was leaving after a visit with Bailey. It seemed trivial to bring it up but she wanted to be as open with Keith as she could.

Keith listened and didn't interrupt her at all. He was quiet once she had finished her frustrating tale. She eventually sat back in the lawn chair and exhaled, relieved she got that weight off her chest. Keith was so quiet Cassie thought maybe he was mad at Jamie or even her. "Thanks for telling me, Cass," was all he said.

"Of course, Keith. Are you upset?" She was almost afraid of the answer but really wanted to air this all out.

"Actually, no. Jamie doesn't worry me and I'm not surprised he's acting or feeling the way he is. You're a catch, Cassie, I've told you this before. He knows he screwed up a good thing." Keith sipped his beer and started at the fire some more.

Okay, she thought. Something seemed off. "Well, I'm glad you understand and aren't upset. But, I have to say, you seem kind of distant, are you sure you're okay?"

Keith sat straighter in his chair, too, and while looking into the fire said, "To be honest, I'm relieved by what you told me. When you said you needed to talk to me about something you sounded so serious that I assumed it had to do with Brian."

Cassie didn't know what to say. She could tell what he was saying even though he didn't say the exact words. He was worried that Brian was still in the picture.

"Keith, are you still concerned about Brian? Are you still thinking he and I have some sort of thing going on?"

"I'm not worried, Cass. I'm just realistic. I've seen the way he looks at you and I saw the way you were when he left for London. When he first left you seemed cranky and almost miserable, like you lost a best friend. And maybe you did. Maybe that was the extent of it, I don't know. I'm really not sure what went on with you and Brian, ever, and I don't think I want to know but I'm really glad he moved. And I hate that I have to be glad that he moved. I should be more confident in our relationship but I feel that he's almost a wedge between us. He's a great guy, I really do like him, but….. I don't know……" Keith's voice kind of trailed off at the end, leaving Cassie feeling smacked in the head that he had felt this way for so long. She also felt a little defensive for Brian but didn't want Keith to know that.

"Keith, I don't know what to say." She practically whispered.

"Don't, Cass, don't say anything. There really isn't anything to say to make me feel better. I really don't feel as bad as I just sounded but these thoughts have popped in my head time to time. I just love you and wish I felt that you loved me just as much."

Cassie felt like a piece of shit. She didn't realize how much Keith had seen between her and Brian. She always thought she had played it cool when he was around the two of them. Since Brian left she finally thought less and less of their kiss and what they said to each other that crazy night. She had no choice but to think of it less. He was in another country. Another time zone. He was with Jane. She was with Keith. Jamie was a loose cannon. She and Brian being together would hurt too many people. This was something she always knew. And, repeating in her head was the question of who's to say that they'd even be a good couple?

She had to let any thoughts of Brian go. They weren't even together and the pain she heard in Keith's voice tore at her heart. She loved Keith. She knew she didn't love him with a crazy, overwhelming, I can't wait to see him kind of love, but she did love him. He was safe. He was good to her and wonderful to Bailey. At the very least, she once again realized she needed to focus more on Keith and their relationship and her feelings for him. He noticed more than she gave him credit for and she wanted their relationship to work.

"Keith, listen, I heard what you said and what you didn't say and I'm sorry you feel the way you do. I know I'm to blame and please know that I didn't mean to hurt you," she said to him while staring at the fire. "I don't really want to talk about Brian but if you want to or have any questions then I will. But all I want to do right now is enjoy this nice evening with you and spend time on our relationship; which makes me very happy."

She reached for his hand and tugged on it so he'd look at her. He eventually did and she looked at him intently and then smiled at him. He smiled back and both of them leaned in for a kiss, their chairs close enough to each other, probably positioned perfectly for such a task by Keith, the most romantic man she knew, and shared a sweet moment of affection and appreciation. He did make her happy, he really did. But she couldn't help but notice her lack of heavy romantic feelings towards him. She hoped those feelings would come with time but she just wasn't sure.

Chapter 23

Cassie didn't want to think about Brian anymore. It was taking too much effort to keep him out of her mind and she was growing frustrated. She had started to get mad at Brian and he technically hadn't done anything. It had been a long time since he went to London and the only contact she had with him were a few group emails Pepper sent to him, Jamie and Cassie with pictures of the kids that she took while babysitting. Any replies from Brian were general comments on how big they were getting and how much he missed them. While she had been annoyed that he hadn't reached out directly to her she was finally making a successful effort to let Brian, or the thought of a relationship with him, go. It definitely took a lot of strength but she knew she had no choice.

Keith was wonderful and attentive and while she appreciated him she still wasn't feeling the desire she wanted to feel for him. She enjoyed spending time with him and they had great conversations, but something was lacking. Their relationship was strong, she supposed, but it hadn't been going the way she had anticipated it would. Maybe she just needed more time. Keith was a great catch so why couldn't she feel the same way towards him that he felt for her? She was definitely growing frustrated with herself. It had been weeks since she decided to make yet another effort on their relationship but she eventually started to realize that she hadn't done much to help move things along. She felt stagnant. And she could tell that Keith was starting to notice. Oh boy.

To add to her frustration, Jamie had eventually come around too often with a stupid smirk on his face as if the two of them had a secret that no one else knew about. There was no secret. She told him this again and again but he kept saying with a sing-song voice that she'd change her mind and want him back. His cockiness was pissing her off to say the least.

One weekend night, Cassie decided to have an impromptu cook out on the grill and basically everyone but, obviously, Brian and Jane, came over. In attendance were Joe and Jack, Pepper and her husband, Cassie's parents, Jamie, Cindy and Lilly, a few co-workers and of course Bailey and Keith. Even Jamie and Cindy's real estate agent, Laurie, had come which Cassie found sort of strange. Thank God, it turned out that Cindy wanted to move (alleluia!) and Jamie really had no say since the house was Cindy's after all. Their agent was someone Cindy knew from her gym so they were basically friends to start.

Jamie was being annoying as ever to Cassie and tried too many times to hug her from behind while she was in the kitchen gathering more food to bring outside. He was being so stupid it was like he wanted to get caught by Cindy and a huge part of Cassie wanted that, too. She kept having to squirm away but finally Cindy walked in and saw what was happening. Both Jamie and Cassie saw Cindy at the same time and Jamie stopped in his tracks. Cassie continued to gather items and said, "Thank God you're here, get him away from me," and walked out. After a while Cindy came outside and sat near Laurie and the two of them went into a deep conversation. Jamie came out a few moments later with a beer in his hand and sat by his parents looking not too happy. She didn't know if anyone else noticed them but Keith eventually whispered to Cassie and asked if something had gone on and she told him. Both of them were glad that it happened because Jamie needed to stop the madness. For a moment Cassie actually felt bad for Cindy. But the moment passed.

Chapter 24

A few days after the cook-out Pepper had sent a group email to Cassie, Cassie's parents, Jamie and Brian with pictures she had taken that day. They were nice pictures, many of them candid ones, and some really cute ones of Bailey and Lilly playing in the sand box. In one of the pictures, taken before Jamie attacked Cassie in the kitchen, there was a photo of Cassie, Jamie and Bailey. In the photograph, Cassie and Jamie had been looking at each other and were laughing at something Bailey had done while sitting between them on the ground with a toy. It was a really nice picture of the three of them. Granted, Cassie wasn't about to print it up and hang on her bedroom wall but thought she may put it in Bailey's room with a few other pictures Pepper had sent.

As usual, Brian replied with his nice comments of how big the kids were getting and how nice it was for everyone to spend time together. Then, his last sentence in his reply email blew Cassie away. He wrote, "*It looks like Jamie and Cassie are really happy, good for them.*" What the-?! What did he mean by that? That Jamie and Cassie look happy TOGETHER or happy in general as if on their own, separate from each other, they are happy people? What did he mean by that? Why would he say that?

She wanted to reply and say, "HUH?" But she didn't. She didn't do anything. She simply sat there reading that sentence over and over again until she heard Bailey waking up from his nap and crying for her from his crib.

Cassie didn't really know what to think of Brian's comment yet didn't want to reach out and ask him. She realized she was scared to talk to him one on one. She had been trying hard to get him out of her system and his being across the pond, out of sight, was a huge help. To talk to him, hear his voice, have that distance disappear across a phone line… well, she wasn't ready for that. Maybe an email would be okay but then that could easily turn into something intimate, romantic, sweet. Or not. She was scared anyway she looked at it and that bothered her.

Jamie came by later that week to take Bailey to the zoo with Lilly. Thankfully he wasn't acting weird nor did he have that look on his face that annoyed Cassie to no end. She figured Cindy chewed him out the other night after she caught him in the act of clawing at Cassie in the kitchen. Although, when she thought back on it, Cindy didn't seem mad. She hadn't seemed happy, per say, but she also did not freak out like Cassie thought she would. And Cassie had enough on her mind so didn't really care either way.

"Hey," Jamie said as she let him in the front door. He had Lilly with him and put her in the playpen with Bailey, lovingly rubbing both their heads.

"Hey, how's it going?" Cassie asked coldly.

"Eh, alright I guess. Cindy and I got into a huge fight the other night. I guess I had it coming. She ended up going to Laurie's house for a few nights to get away from me. From us." He walked away from the babies towards the kitchen.

"What do you mean?" Cassie was following him, wondering why she even cared to ask.

"I don't know, Cass. She's been acting weird lately. It seems like she doesn't want to settle down and be an official family now. I guess I don't act that way a lot either. I don't even know if it's what I want with her. If I've ever wanted that with her," he said while walking around running his hands through his hair

He eventually continued and said, "Neither one of us seems happy with the other. I guess we just need some time apart. I don't know. I really don't know."

Jamie walked over to the kitchen window and looked out, slowly shaking his head, clearly wondering how he got to the position he was in right now. Neither of them spoke for a while. Cassie, once again, felt bad for Jamie and especially felt bad for both of the children. Lilly and Bailey had no idea what was going on right now but at some point, how they each came to be half siblings, well that story would come out. She realized that was probably why she cared about Jamie and Cindy having a fight. She didn't want Bailey or Lilly to have too many step-moms. She wanted Jamie and Cindy to work out as a couple. To be a good couple, to have it make sense for the kids one day why their dad strayed from his first wife. She wanted them to be a strong and happy couple for the children's' sake, and maybe a little of her own. Weird as it sounded, Jamie and Cindy being a love story that had to happen made it a little easier to accept as a reason for why her marriage to Jamie fell apart.

"I'm sorry, Jamie, I really am. Have you tried to talk to her since she left? At least send a text or something?"

"No, not yet. I just want to spend time with the kids and forget about how I got to where I am in life right now. And I'm sorry for acting like such as ass lately. I was just trying to get my old life back," he chuckled softly.

"Yeah, I figured as much," Cassie said gently.

"I wanted things back to the way they were so much I even told my parents and brother that we were getting back together," he said as if it were no big deal.

"What?! Are you serious?" Cassie said, trying to control her voice.

"Yeah, I'm serious. My parents didn't believe me and my mom even said that I needed to see a therapist and get my head on straight. You know how Pepper can tell it like it is," said Jamie calmly. He had no idea how freaked out Cassie was at that moment.

"What did Brian say?" Cassie asked, trying to hide the urgency in her voice. She had to know what Brian said. And it all made sense to her why he commented on the picture of her and Jamie that Pepper had sent to him and his reply of how it was nice to see them together.

"Oh, not much. I caught him in the middle of a business dinner so he had to step outside to take my call. We play phone tag a lot with the time difference. Anyway, the connection wasn't so great but he sounded surprised but happy for me. For us," Jamie said and turned to Cassie. "I think he knew I was crazy, like my mom and dad did, but he didn't want to burst my bubble either."

"Wow, Jamie. That wasn't cool of you to do that. You knew we weren't going to get back together. What if Cindy found out you were saying these things? She would have gone crazy! Did you let them know it wasn't true?" Cassie was mad at Jamie yet relieved to know why Brian wrote what he wrote in that email. She was sort of mad at Brian though, too. She wished he had clarified what Jamie said with her. He could have sent her a separate email or text or called her, to sort of close things between them, if he really thought she and Jamie were getting back together.

"Yeah, I know, Cass. I'm sorry. My parents didn't say anything to Cindy. And Brian doesn't talk to her so it's not like he would have called her to tell her. Plus it wouldn't have been his business. He may have told Jane but it doesn't matter. And, no, I haven't told them it wasn't true mainly because I was embarrassed and figured they knew it wasn't true. Listen," Jamie stepped closer to her, "just know that I really am sorry for acting all crazy and telling people things that weren't true." He sounded truly sorry. And clueless.

"I understand, I guess," Cassie said. She needed to be alone for a little while so wanted Jamie to get going. She brought the conversation back to where he and Cindy needed to get over this recent fight and work on their relationship. She added, "Just a word of advice, Jamie... I'm not sure if you've noticed but Cindy can be high maintenance," she smiled a little as she said it to try and lighten the mood. "So she may be expecting you to make the first move. If you don't, well..."

"Yeah, yeah, I've noticed. I'll try to fix things up," he said defeated.

Chapter 25

Jamie finally left with the kids so Cassie was able to digest what he had told her. Brian thinking that Jamie and she were back together was probably hard for him to hear. Yet he didn't reach out to confirm it with her. Maybe he didn't want to interfere, which would be just like him. She guessed there would be no point because there was not really a relationship between Cassie and Brian to even discuss. But she definitely wanted to let him know it wasn't true. She was nervous to just call him out of the blue. What if Jane was there? Or what if she caught him at a work function like Jamie did? Email would be a good way to reach out to him. But she was nervous.

A glass of wine for courage and a quick sandwich later, Cassie sat in front of the computer and logged on. She didn't know where to begin let alone what to write to him. Since she hadn't checked her home email in a while she had to let the messages load. Unfortunately she received a lot of junk email so this took a while. She saw subject lines such as "How to Tell if Your Spouse is Cheating" (where was that email a few years ago?!), "Please help and send money," and yet another sale at a major department store (you know the one) filled her inbox. She always deleted emails in chunks so once they were finished loading she started to do just that when she saw Brian's name. She stopped and sat back in her chair. The email was sent about a week ago. The subject line read, "From Brian." It almost looked like someone hacked his email and it was a spam message but she clicked on it anyway. The email wasn't spam. At a glance she could see that it was only a few sentences long. She was too afraid to read it but knew she had to, so she leaned forward, and read the email.

She read it twice.

Her eyes filled with tears.

She heard her doorbell ringing.

Chapter 26

Cassie was wiping her eyes as she went downstairs to see who was at the door. She opened it to Jamie and two crying babies.

"What happened?" Cassie asked as she reached for Bailey, rubbing his back as he cried and put his little arm around her neck. Lilly was doing the same to Jamie.

"I forgot their diaper bags so I think they're hungry and need changing. I feel horrible. They started to cry as soon as we got to the zoo. I knew I forgot the bags about halfway into the drive there but figured we wouldn't stay long and I could get them some snacks and maybe juice boxes," he said while looking at Lilly and her sad face. "Wow, can they cry," Jamie said with a small laugh.

Cassie was already in the kitchen getting a snack and juice cups for the children. Bailey drank quickly but he wasn't able to breathe out of his nose from all the crying so couldn't drink the juice fast enough which made him cry even more. Lilly was doing pretty much the same thing but both eventually calmed down and settled into their parents' arms and finished their juice. She and Jamie each fed them pieces of Cheerios which melted in their mouths right away making them want more and more. She grabbed two jars of bananas for them and both she and Jamie fed them quickly. They were famished. She felt bad, too, because she didn't realize Bailey was so hungry when he left. She wasn't getting a Mom of the Year award that day.

"Aw, man," Jamie said. "They were hungry, I feel horrible."

"I know, I do, too. I guess it happens and they're fine now. Let's let them finish this and get them changed, I can tell Bailey needs a fresh diaper and maybe even a bath. Does Lilly?"

"Probably. But I can take her home and give her a quick bath. Actually, let's just change them for now. I'd at least like to take them for a walk to the playground down the street. I didn't really get any quality time with them since we left the zoo right away," Jamie said.

It was still a few hours until Bailey's bedtime so Cassie didn't mind. She and Jamie changed their diapers and Jamie ran next door to get the double stroller he had for times like this. He really was a good dad and she was glad they were able to get along like this and be on the same page when it came to Bailey, and even

Lilly. She hoped he'd find his happiness whether it was with Cindy or someone else. Just not her.

Chapter 27

Jamie left with the kids and Cassie went back to her computer. She read for a third time the email from Brian before she replied. He wrote:

Hey Cass, How are you? I'm sorry I haven't reached out since I've been in London but as you can imagine it's been really busy but I know that isn't an excuse and I'm sorry. Even though I'm in the office most of the time I have seen some local sights and it's really nice here, very old and lots of character. But, anyway, the reason for my email isn't about London. What I'm about to say isn't going to be fair of me (Jamie told me you two are back together) but I have to say this regardless of the response. I miss you. Do you miss me?

Cassie was surprised and happy, to say the least. This was it. This was what she wanted to hear from Brian. He made the first move. Now it was her turn. But she was scared to make a move back. She was worried of what their being together would do to Jamie and Keith, even Bailey. How confusing for the little guy. But at the same time she knew that she wanted to be with Brian, that she missed him more than she thought she would or even could. And here he was, reaching out, taking a chance, thinking maybe it's his last chance, and she hadn't responded yet. She clicked reply and wrote from the heart…..

Brian, I'm sorry that I haven't responded to this email, I haven't checked it in a long time. I'm glad you like London and would love to see any photographs you've taken. Jamie and I are not, nor were we ever, back together. He misspoke and was going through a bad time. He seems better now. And….I miss you, too.

She wasn't sure what else to say and figured he probably wouldn't know what to say either, so she clicked the send button, and then sat there and held her breath.

Chapter 28

Cassie sat at her computer after she sent the reply to Brian for a long time. She was hoping he'd see the email right away and reply but also knew he probably wouldn't. After a while Jamie came back with Bailey and she was happily distracted with getting him ready for bed and reading him some bedtime stories. She knew she would check her email too many times for the rest of the night and days to come.

For the next few days Cassie checked her email like a mad woman. She was anxious to hear from Brian so tried to keep busy. Weighing heavy on her mind was Keith. She hadn't seen him for almost a full week because of his intense travel schedule and being out of town so much. The last time they saw each other she thought things were good. But oddly the few times he called over the past week the conversation seemed strained and not very enjoyable. He didn't know about the emails between her and Brian so it was a little mysterious why he wasn't acting like his usual self. Regardless, she had to end it with Keith. She didn't want to hurt him but had to do something. Even if nothing came from the emails she and Brian shared she knew it wasn't fair to Keith to drag him along, his thinking they were going in a forward direction when in reality she felt much less romance between them as the days went on.

On a side note something big seemed to be going on Jamie and Cindy. All they did was argue. Jamie had told Cassie he wanted to work on his relationship with Cindy but whatever he was doing wasn't working. Jamie and Cindy didn't seem to be improving their relationship and the unfortunate times that Cassie saw Cindy, Cindy barely said a word to her let alone a mean one. She seemed different lately, even less annoying and less flirtation with everyone from Keith to the mailman.

The more Cassie thought about it the more she realized that Cindy wasn't as annoying as she used to be. She wasn't necessarily nice but she wasn't as mean. And Cindy had always wanted to be the center of attention where men were involved but she seemed to be less flirtation, more mellow. Cassie presumed she was simply maturing and was glad to see it, especially for Lilly's sake, but also for her and Jamie. Although, while she seemed less bothersome she still got her fire lit when Jamie was around. The two of them just didn't seem to get along.

One day, while Cassie had been doing some yard work Cindy came outside and sat on a chair with her face to the sun. Cassie ignored her since she seemed to be relaxing but Cindy actually started a conversation with her.

"Hey, Cassie, have you ever been in love?" Cindy asked, still keeping her eyes closed and face to the sun.

Cassie gave her an odd look, which Cindy couldn't see, and replied that she had. "Well, yes, with Jamie, of course."

"I know that. I mean besides him."

"Oh, well, not really." Cassie replied although her first thought was of Brian. Then her second was of Keith! "Well, aside from Jamie and Keith, not really," she practically said in one breath. She internally panicked wondering why she didn't say Keith's name immediately. Cassie did care deeply for Keith, of course she did. Their relationship seemed to be a good one but mainly from Keith's efforts. It never seemed to move onto a "next step" level but Cassie wanted it that way, she didn't want to have him move in, or get married, or even get engaged. She enjoyed her simple evenings when Keith wasn't there with Bailey.

"Yeah, I figured you were in love with Keith. I just meant anyone else, maybe anyone else that you kind of shouldn't be in love with," Cindy replied cryptically, still keeping her eyes closed.

"Why do you want to know?" Cassie wasn't about to share her feelings for Brian with Cindy. No way.

"Oh, I don't know, I'm just wondering. It's a good feeling to be in love, especially in the beginning of the relationship. But sometimes you wonder if it's right, if it's okay to feel that way about another person."

"Why would you wonder if it's okay to love someone?" Cassie asked. Cindy was being evasive and Cassie was ready to go back in the house and check to see if Bailey was up from his nap yet even though she knew he wasn't because she had the baby monitor near her. She kind of wanted to get out of there and away from their weird conversation. Yet, at the same time, she couldn't pull herself away.

"Oh, I don't know. If you had loved someone that wasn't right for you or someone maybe your friends didn't approve of, I wondered if you cared, you know, like if it made a difference to you. If it mattered enough to *not* have a relationship with that person," Cindy finally turned away from the sun, and opened her eyes, blinking to readjust her focus.

Cassie wondered if Cindy knew about her feelings for Brian. How could she know? She knew Brian wouldn't tell her and he definitely wasn't going to tell Jamie. Joe would never betray her trust and Keith would never confide any concerns to Cindy. So where was this coming from? She wasn't about to share any secret of sorts with Cindy of all people.

"Sorry, Cindy, I guess I can't help you with that question. But I have to ask, are you asking because you loved Jamie when he had been my husband?" Yeah, she went there. "Are you feeling bad about that?" Cassie was asking a bold question but felt maybe Cindy was finally starting to humanize and make amends. Although it sure didn't seem like Cindy even liked Jamie much lately but Cassie didn't really know what went on behind closed doors.

"Oh, no," Cindy almost laughed. "No, not at all." She waved her hand as if to shoo away such a silly thought. She surprisingly realized how bitchy she was being and sort of stopped in her tracks. "But I mean, I know that was wrong, I do. But I wasn't talking about that." Cassie thought that was nice of her to say but noticed she still didn't apologize. Even though Cindy seemed different, there was still a lot of the old Cindy inside.

"Okay, then, why are you asking this?" Cassie was ready to close up this meaningless conversation and get back to her yard work before Bailey woke up. She really had no time for an annoying line of questions.

Cindy started to pick up her chair and move to her back porch, away from Cassie in the front yard, and simply said, "Oh, no reason." And with that she put her chair on the back deck and went inside her house leaving Cassie to wonder how long it would take for Cindy and Jamie to sell that house and move. It couldn't happen soon enough.

Chapter 29

Cassie still hadn't heard from Brian and was starting to wonder if he had moved on. She knew that Brian wasn't an email kind of guy, barely a texting kind of guy, so figured he hadn't seen her reply yet. But the better part of a week had gone by and she found herself running out of excuses for why he hadn't gotten back in touch with her. Once again she tried to put Brian out of her mind.

Keith had been traveling quite a bit for close to a month with many times only being back in town on the weekends for barely a few hours. She missed him but more as a friend to hang out with. Breaking up with him wasn't something she wanted to do over the phone but since they hadn't spent much time together she had to wait for the right time when he wasn't running out the door to catch a flight. She was glad for him to see his career going so well and knew he was a positive difference at the company. Cassie didn't work with him on projects anymore but that was fine with her. Too much time with your significant other personally AND at work was too much time with your significant other.

Keith finally had a small break in his schedule and asked Cassie out to dinner. She brought Bailey to her parents for the night so she was able to take her time getting ready and knew she wouldn't have to rush through dinner to get back home to relieve them. She wasn't sure how the break-up conversation would go and didn't want to worry about getting back by a certain time.

That night Keith picked her up and looked as handsome as ever. He gave her a hug and quick kiss on the lips. She was surprised he didn't give her a longer kiss since they hadn't really seen each other in a while but that was okay with her. And she figured he probably needed to get settled and back in the swing of things. Traveling too much can really throw off someone's typical behaviors until they adjust to being home again or back in the office for full days.

"Hey, you ready?" He asked, barely looking at her. He usually gave a compliment but this time wanted to get going.

"Yeah, sure, let me get my purse." When she came back to the door he was already getting in his car. He usually waited and walked with her to the car. She realized she was nitpicking and didn't want to do that especially since she was about to break his heart. She just shrugged his behavior off and focused on the night ahead, wondering how it would go.

They went to a new place called, "The Deck." It was a cute little restaurant and bar with a large outdoor deck that overlooked a river wide enough for various people to sail, kayak, and row and take a dinner cruise on all at the same time. The sun was setting so torches were lit as well cute little hanging white lights. On the deck there were many tables with lit candles on each one and a large fire pit to the side with chairs around it for whoever wanted to sit there and unwind. It was a really relaxing place to be and she hoped that they would have a nice time. Even though she was about to break his heart.

Their waitress came and took their drink orders and they looked over the menus, not really saying much to each other. Cassie decided to break the ice and asked if he was glad to be back and not have to travel for a while.

"Yeah, it's nice to be home," he said not too convincingly and then took a long sip of his drink.

"Well, I'm glad you're back." She smiled at him, taking a long sip of her drink, too. Is this how the evening was going to go? Yikes.

They didn't talk anymore until the waitress came and took their orders. She brought them another round of drinks since the first went down so quickly and they continued to sit in silence looking out at the water and all the activity going on.

"So," they both said at the same time. They both laughed lightly but Cassie didn't continue. She wanted to see what he had to say.

"So," he repeated, "I need to talk to you about something."

"Okay…," she said slowly wondering what he wanted to say to her. *Oh no*, she thought, *he knows*.

He leaned toward her and said, "Well, you know I've been traveling a lot lately and barely had time to see you and Bailey. I first want to apologize for that," he reached across the table and held both his hands over hers.

She looked down and their hands a little confused. "It's okay. I understand," she said.

"Well," he let go of her hands and leaned back in his chair. He took another long sip of his beer. "The second thing I wanted to say is...," he said with his voice drifting off.

"Keith, what's up?" Cassie asked, growing a little annoyed.

"I've met someone," he said.

"What? How?" Asked Cassie after a long moment of silence. She knew she really had no right to ask and that his answers didn't really make a difference but she had to know.

"I'm sorry, Cass," Keith said sadly. The waitress came over with their food and both sat silently while she put plates down and took away the empty drink glasses. She told them to wave her down if they needed anything, seeming fully aware that she caught them in the middle of a serious talk. Oh yeah she did.

Neither touched their food and just looked at each other for a few moments.

"She's someone I know from grad school. She works in one of the client offices I've been working with for the past few months," he said.

"So, you're telling me that this has been going on for months?" Cassie asked. That didn't make sense, he seemed so focused on their relationship. How could he have someone on the side?

"Well, no, not really. Yeah, I first saw her a few months ago but nothing happened. We went to dinner a few times since I was out there for weeks at a time but that was all," he said earnestly.

"Okay, so how or when did it turn into more?" Given that she was about to break things off with him anyway she really had no right to ask him anything. A big part of her was glad he found someone while another part of her, the unjustified part, was kind of pissed.

"Oh, I don't know, Cass," he said as he exhaled. "Things just happened. You and I weren't clicking anymore. I tried real hard to keep our relationship moving forward but it just wasn't. I don't know if it was because I starting to have feelings for someone else or because you seemed hard to get close to. I don't know. I just know that I'm sorry," he said sincerely.

He looked down at his food and then out to the water. He looked like a lost soul. She suddenly felt bad for him. Her lack of enthusiasm and obviously lack of commitment to their relationship probably pushed him into another woman's arms. She was as much to blame as anyone.

She didn't feel mad anymore. She felt relieved and happy for him. And she felt a weight lifted off her shoulders, too. Reaching across the table to grab his hands, she said, "Keith, I get it and I don't blame you. And you weren't imagining things. I wasn't trying as hard as I wanted to for our relationship to progress. You're a great guy. One of the best I've ever met. But for some reason, I wasn't feeling things that any other woman in the world would. And I'm sorry, too," she looked him directly in the eye so he could see just how sorry she was.

Both leaned towards each other with tears in their eyes and did a last squeeze of each other's hands and let go. They sat back in their seats, looking both sad yet content. "Well, do you want to stay here and eat or head back? I'm okay either way," Keith said.

"You know, I think I want to finish our meal and enjoy this view. And maybe by dessert I'll want to hear more about this woman who took you away from me," she said with a smile.

Chapter 30

The rest of their meal went by nicely. She really was going to miss him as a friend. His new relationship with the new woman, Laney, sounded pretty advanced for such a short period of time. Maybe it was because they knew each other already, Cassie wasn't sure. As it turned out, he had plans to interview at a company that was also in the same city as Laney. Keith sure had been busy. How did she not notice when the men in her life found someone else?

He took her home after dinner and gave her a long hug at the door. "I'm going to miss you," Cassie said sadly.

Keith pulled away, looked at her and said, "I'm going to miss you, too." He kissed her softly on the lips. It was nice and perfect. "I miss Bailey already. Can we please try and stay in touch? I'd love to know how he's doing and know that you're doing well. Which I know you will be fine." She agreed and knew their comments weren't just a thing to say. They did care about the other deeply and wanted to keep in touch. They hugged again and he pulled back, gave her one final look and left. She watched him drive away and wasn't sure what she felt. Sad or happy? She didn't know. But she definitely felt at ease.

Since Bailey was at her parents' house she took a long, hot bath and opened a bottle of wine. As she sat soaking in the tub, she realized she never told Keith about her feelings for Brian. That was probably for the best, she figured. She didn't want Keith, or herself, to think she was breaking up with him because Brian was in the picture. It wasn't about Brian. Plus she hadn't heard back from Brian anyway. Cassie was unexpectedly a woman with no man in her life. She went from two great guys to zippo. But, that was okay. She knew she and Bailey would be fine with or without her having a special someone. But it sure would be a nice bonus.

After her relaxing bath she put on her most comfy pajamas and had another glass of wine. She was going to start reading a book she had bought so long ago but hadn't had time to read. As soon as she sat on the couch with Sophie she heard a knock at the front door.

She looked through the peep hole and saw Jamie standing there. She opened the door and asked what he wanted all at the same time.

"I'm sorry it's so late, Cass. I didn't know where else to go," he said and walked past her into the living room.

"Come in," she said dryly and shut the door. "What's up?"

"Cindy and I are done, over, finished. She's been seeing someone she met at her gym and finally told me. I have no idea who it is but guess it doesn't matter anyway," he went into the kitchen and helped himself to a glass of wine from the bottle she had opened.

"I'm sorry, Jamie. I'm not surprised though. You two have been fighting like cats and dogs for months."

"Yeah, I know, I know. I'm not really bummed though. I wanted things to work out but probably only because I ruined *our* marriage and didn't want another failed marriage. Plus Lilly. So now I have two kids who I let down," he said sincerely.

"Oh, Jamie, don't beat yourself up over this. Just let things settle down. The kids are both too young to know anything or ask any questions so you've got time to figure everything out. Don't think so far into the future," she told him.

"You're right, Cass. I just need to step back and take some time for myself. Man, I'm glad Cindy and I didn't get married. That would have just made it worse. So technically I've only been divorced once," he said happily. Uh, ok, sure.

"Yep, you're good to go, Jaime," she said with a hint of sarcasm.

"Alright, well, I've got to get going. I need to find a place to stay for a few days. Know of anywhere I can go?" He looked around the house and Cassie realized he was asking to stay there!

"Uh, no, you lunatic," she said firmly.

"Funny. Fine, I had to ask. I have a key to Brian's place. I'll just go over there," he said.

"What place? I thought his company found a renter for his apartment when he went to London," Cassie said.

"Oh, yeah, that's true and his office was taking care of all of that. But I guess the person that was renting the place had to move, too, so his apartment has been sitting empty for a few weeks," Jamie informed her.

"Are you sure? Does Brian know you're going to stay there," she asked.

"Yeah. I talked to Brian the other day and he said the guy had to bail cause of a job transfer so all is clear. I don't know the details. Anyway, all I know is that it's vacant so I'll stay over there for a while."

"You talked to Brian?" Cassie asked too desperately.

"Yeah, the other day. And don't worry, I told him you and I weren't back together," he said as if a second thought. He was looking through her pantry for some food and not really paying attention to her. She was glad because she probably looked guilty of something.

"What did he say?" Her voice was more controlled than she felt, thank God. She didn't want Jamie to pick up on any of her Brian vibes.

"What do you mean?" He asked over his shoulder.

"I don't know. Like, was he glad?" She said but never should have said. Shit.

Jamie pulled his head out of the pantry and looked at her. "Why would he be glad we weren't together?"

"Oh, um, I don't know. I'm just wondering what he said," she fumbled with the words.

Jamie looked at her for a while then asked, "Is there something going on with you and Brian?"

Shit again.

"Jamie, Brian's in London. How could something be going on?" She asked somewhat defiantly.

"I don't know but you're acting weird. And so did he when I told him you and I weren't really back together," he said slowly.

She had to know what Brian said but knew if she asked again Jamie would freak out. She tried a new tactic. "Well, I don't know how Brian acted when you told him the truth. You basically told a huge lie to your parents and brother. I'm sure your parents weren't happy with you when you told them you had been lying. So it makes sense to me that Brian was probably mad, too." She could really pull things out of her ass.

"No, Cass. He wasn't mad. If anything he asked too many questions like you are. He wanted to know if I was serious or joking. And HE wanted to know if YOU knew that I had lied about things. What the hell is going on with you two?" He was getting mad and that was the last thing she or he needed.

"Jamie, relax. Calm down. Sit down." She led him to the couch and sat down next to him. He looked at her like he was a little kid having a fit. He took a long sip of his wine and wiped his mouth with the back of his hand. Looking at him she saw a glimpse of Bailey in his face, when Bailey's frustrated with something. The look was cuter on Bailey.

She wasn't sure how she was going to approach this or even if she should, but she was put in a figurative corner so had to do something. "Jamie, listen. Brian and I had gotten really close when I was pregnant with Bailey. You had just left me for Cindy, she and I were both pregnant, and I was pretty miserable. He was a real friend to me when my world crashed in front of my eyes," she looked at him indicating that he was the reason she was so upset. He knew. And she was glad. He needed to hear of the consequences to his actions. It would help him make better choices in the long run, especially since he couldn't make it work with Cindy.

"And I'm not blaming you, Jamie, not completely anyway, but you have to know that I needed someone and he was there. Nothing happened with us. We were friends. Good friends. After Bailey was born and I started to feel whole again, Brian and I were sort of at a cross roads. We didn't take our relationship past a friendship but I do think we both considered it," she said as gently as she could.

Jamie wasn't saying anything but he was definitely listening. She continued.

"Around that time Keith and I started to have a relationship and Brian was seeing people and then eventually Jane. We sort of just let the friendship go because we didn't want to push things. While the friendship was important to us we sort of didn't have time for it anymore cause of everyday life. I had a baby and a new relationship with Keith and he had a busy career and a new girlfriend. To be honest, I didn't really want to have a relationship with Keith but he was there. He was a great guy and we had a good time at first but my feelings for him weren't progressing like that should have. As a matter of fact he and I just broke up," she said.

"Oh," Jamie said simply. "I'm sorry, Cass. I really liked him. He was good with Bailey."

"Thanks, Jamie. I really liked him, too, but that was all. I never really felt more than that," Cassie said sadly. She really did wish she felt more for Keith but it was what it was.

"So, anyway," she inhaled and sat back on the couch, "here we are."

Jamie just sat with his wine glass in his hands, turning it every which way watching the wine roll around inside.

"Jamie, I'm not saying I don't have feelings for Brian. I really don't know what I'm feeling but it doesn't matter because he isn't here. He's in London and he's with Jane."

"No, he isn't, they broke up," Jamie said turning to look at Cassie.

"Oh. They did?" Replied Cassie in a slow, high pitched voice she didn't recognize as her own.

"Nice cover, Cass. I know you. You're smiling on the inside."

"No! I'm not," she said with an attempt at being genuine. She didn't want Brian or Jane heartbroken but being honest with herself, she was happy that they were no longer together.

"Cassie, listen. I just want you to be happy. And I want my brother to be happy. I don't really want you guys happy together but I have no room to judge things or stand in your way. Just, I don't know…if you two do decide to take it to beyond a friendship, don't flaunt it in front of me. Okay?" He looked down at his wineglass and feel silent.

Cassie could tell Jamie meant what he said and that, while not his first choice, would learn to live with her and Brian if they decided to be more than friends. She didn't know if that would ever happen but was glad she had been honest with Jamie.

"Okay," she said and gave Jamie a little nudge on his arm. A hug didn't seem the right thing to do, especially considering he was giving her and his brother permission to do whatever, but she didn't know what else to do.

Jamie eventually left and Cassie began reading her new book but soon after became too tired. She started to turn off lights and head upstairs to bed when she heard another soft knock on the front door.

Figuring it was Jamie again she didn't look through the peep hole and opened the door to surprisingly find Brian standing there. Brian. Standing there. Looking jet lagged and exhausted with a carry-on duffle bag slung over his shoulder and a single piece of luggage and a briefcase on the ground at his feet. He had on a sports coat, shirt, loosened tie and dress slacks and shoes. A taxi cab was on the street slowly pulling away. She couldn't believe he was standing there.

"Brian," she said softly.

"Cass," he said, barely a whisper.

They stood and looked at each other not sure what to do or say. At that moment, a moment she may never forget, she realized her future was standing before her. She was a woman happy with her own self and child. She was self-sufficient, educated and strong. But here before her was the missing piece. The piece of her life that made her extra happy, extra content, extra peaceful. She realized she had no idea how much Brian meant to her until that moment.

He looked at her in a mirror-like way. As if he was standing there waiting for her to make him whole, make him happy, make him smile. They both looked at each other.

Then he slowly picked up his things and walked towards her. He stepped into the foyer and put everything on the floor. He shut the door. He slowly took off his jacket. All the while looking at her, in her eyes, at her lips, at her pajamas. Her yellow duck printed pajamas. Yep. But she didn't care. He didn't either. He started to smile that slow, sexy smile of his and grabbed her by the waist, pulled her toward him, and kissed her. And after a moment of sheer surprise and disbelief she kissed him back.

Epilogue

"Mommy, juice peezze?" Bailey said in his adorable two year old voice.

"Hang on, Bay. Mommy's getting your cake out of the oven. I need to decorate it later for your birthday party," Cassie said happily. She put the cake on the counter to cool down, took off the oven mitts and poured Bailey some juice in his sippy cup and put it on the tray on his high chair. He had eaten most of his breakfast and was gearing up to go play outside. He was a ball of energy, a typical little boy. Anything to do with sports he liked. The backyard was full of plastic baseballs and bats, footballs, Frisbees and a small basketball hoop and ball. Cassie loved to watch him try to hit the ball off the tee with his little bat or try to shoot the ball into the basket. Whether he made it or not he'd smile and do it again. He was at a great age and she was trying to enjoy every minute she could.

"Lilly, Mommy?" Bailey wanted to know if his sister was coming over to play with him. She was and told him so. Cindy would be over soon with Lilly and then she was taking the two of them to the playground while Cassie got things ready for Bailey's birthday party.

She wiped Bailey's mouth and face and carried him upstairs to his room to change him into his play clothes. He liked to pick out his clothes and she let him. Often it was an interesting match of top and bottom but that didn't matter. He was making choices and Cassie knew it was a huge life lesson, of many, for him to learn.

As she helped Bailey put on his shoes she heard the bathroom shower turn off. From Bailey's room she could see into her bedroom and the attached bath. And that meant she could also see Brian coming out of the bathroom with a towel around his waist, his wet hair all in disarray and his wonderful physique glistening from the shower water. After all this time he still stopped her in her tracks. *Woah*, she thought.

"Mommy?" Asked Bailey ever so innocently.

"Oh, sorry, Bay." Mommy was just checking out your Uncle Brian. She helped Bailey finish getting ready for his day and carried him back downstairs to the play room. She ended up converting the den into a playroom area since they rarely ate at the formal table. All too soon Bailey would be grown up and no longer need a play area. So sacrificing a dining room was a no brainer. She sat and played with him for a bit until she heard someone knocking on the front door. She opened it to find Cindy standing there.

"Hey," they both said at the same time.

"Is Bailey ready? I wanted to go to the park with them now because we have a showing later today before Bailey's party. We're trying to squeeze in all the business we can before the baby comes," Cindy said happily. Past Cindy, waddling across the yard towards them was Laurie, her realtor friend, with Lilly running ahead of her. Cindy scooped down to pick up Lilly and reached over to give Laurie a kiss. Didn't see that coming, did you?

"Hey, guys. Sorry it took me so long to get here," she said while rubbing her stomach. Laurie was a small person so even though she was only 6 months pregnant she looked like she was about to start pushing the baby out any moment.

"No problem. How're you feeling?" Cassie asked. Before Laurie and Cindy got together, Laurie had been married but her husband cheated on her. A lot. They divorced and after a while they tried to rekindle things. But he kept cheating. During the rekindling timeframe Laurie got pregnant. So just like Cassie had been Laurie was freshly pregnant and divorced. Cindy and she became close after they met at the gym and the rest is history.

"I feel good overall but definitely am tired a lot. All this extra work to build up business before we take off some time when the baby comes is adding up. I'm glad Cindy finally got her Realtor's License though. That's definitely helpful so she can do some of the showings. Did she tell you we have one later today? But don't worry, we'll be back in plenty of time for Bailey's party," she said with a smile.

Cassie really liked Laurie. And she actually liked Cindy again. Cindy had never sold her house so still lived next door. It made Cassie chuckle when she thought of how at one point she wished more than anything that Cindy would sell her house and she and Jamie would move. Now, she was glad they didn't. Once Cindy and Laurie finally broke their barriers and turned into more than just friends Cindy was practically a different person.

As it turned out all her man problems and constant irritability was because she was so unhappy. Cindy was basically a huge flirt and needed a man's attention to fill a void she didn't even know was there. But Laurie made her truly happy. And Cassie was pleased for both of them and especially for Lilly. She seemed so much happier than the days of when Jamie and Cindy would fight constantly. It was a win-win for everyone.

Cindy, Laurie and the kids went to the playground while Cassie readied the house for the party. The guest list was the same as Bailey's first birthday minus Jane and Keith. Both were in new relationships and both moved to different areas. Keith a few states over and Jane to Paris according to mutual friends. Keith had a new job and now traveled internationally. And he was still seeing the "other woman" he knew from grad school, Laney. He seemed to be doing well. And she figured Jane was thrilled to be in Paris, the fashion world mecca. They were both doing well which was all she and Brian wanted for them.

Joe and Jack were on the guest list and she looked forward to seeing them. They had come back from their honeymoon a week before and Cassie had been looking forward to hearing all of their stories and seeing pictures. And she knew both her parents and Brian's parents liked to hear Joe's extravagant stories, too. His stories were blunt to the point of people blushing, especially her mom and Pepper. Yes, Joe was definitely entertaining. He and Jack were a good couple; Joe being over the top with almost all that he did and Jack being more conservative and grounded. They both complimented each other nicely.

And Jamie was doing well. He had a girlfriend of a few good months named Annie. She was also divorced and had a sweet little 3 year old son named Alex. Jamie, Annie and all the kids often went to the zoo and the playground together. Cassie liked that Annie was so good with Bailey and Lilly.

Annie was the Head Chef and part owner at a very upscale restaurant in the city and provided a good living for her and Alex. She seemed to make Jamie laugh a lot and he seemed very smitten with her. He took the news of Brian and Cassie well, most likely because he had a heads up that something may happen. Jamie wasn't the best husband to Cassie yet he did love her so it was hard for him to see her and Brian together. But he was getting used to it and handling things well not only with them but with his own life. He was starting to grow up and Cassie was proud of him.

As Cassie was decorating the cake she once again marveled at how different her life was from a few years ago. She was proud of herself that she made it through a stormy time in her life and came out stronger and happier. Anything can happen and she was very thankful she had her friends, family and inner strength to get thorough the rough patches. And most importantly Bailey was thriving and well adjusted. Sure, she will have some unique stories to tell him about how he and his sister came to be and how his uncle became his step-dad. Oh yeah. But that story telling was all for another day. For now, Cassie couldn't be any happier or excited for the future.

Brian came in from the backyard where he had been putting up balloons and setting up some tables and chairs. He had on an old Clemson t-shirt, athletic shorts and running shoes. He looked good. He went up to Cassie as she was frosting the cake and gave her a kiss. Then he simply went back outside again. She smiled. He often stopped what he was doing just to give her a kiss. He brought her flowers. He left post-it notes on the counter with "oxo" written on them. He played with Bailey and Lilly and read to them at night. He was good with them.

And his job was still strong. The new office in London was running smoothly and his boss had been impressed with all that Brian did for them overseas. Brian's old job was waiting for him when he moved back to the U.S. and after a while he was promoted to a Senior Partner role.

All was good for both Brian and Cassie. He was happy. And so was she.

Made in the USA
Lexington, KY
11 August 2016